T A I N

SHIRE

HISTORIC BRITAIN

NOTTINGHAMSHIRE

MIKE ABRAHAMSON

The
History
Press

First published 2010

The History Press
The Mill, Brimscombe Port
Stroud, Gloucestershire, GL5 2QG
www.thehistorypress.co.uk

British Library Cataloguing in Publication Data.
A catalogue record for this book is available from the British Library.

ISBN 978 0 7524 5352 1

Typesetting and origination by The History Press
Printed in India by Nutech Print Services

ACKNOWLEDGEMENTS

I would like to thank the staff at the Local Studies Library, Nottingham, for their ever-ready help and expertise. It is an excellent source for local history and those researching their family tree. Thank you to all those people involved with the various sites mentioned here (and some that didn't make the pages because of space constraints) who gave me their time generously.

I would also like to thank Cate Ludlow at The History Press for her help, advice and encouragement. It helped form a raw idea into something publishable. I alone, however, take responsibility for any errors that may still reside in the pages.

Thank you for buying this copy and I hope very much that you find it enjoyable and that it helps to stimulate your interest in local and national history.

Finally, a big thank you to my wife, Elaine, who is not a historian but has read many of the chapters many times. If she found them interesting, I knew I was on the right lines.

PICTURE CREDITS

Thank you to Nottinghamshire County Council, Nottingham City Council and A. McArthur, who have kindly allowed me to reproduce images from Picture the Past – www.picturethepast.org.uk. This excellent, not-for-profit project has thousands of archive pictures from the library and museum collections of Derby, Derbyshire, Nottingham and Nottinghamshire, freely available online.

Image NTGM009692 – Courtesy of A. McArthur and www.picturethepast.org.uk.

Images NTGM002829, NTGM008717, NTGM009111, NTGM009727, NTGM010238, NTGM010366, NTGM011015, NTGM011313 – Courtesy of Nottingham City Council and www.picturethepast.org.uk.

Images NCCE003336, NCCN000930, NCCN000932 – courtesy of Nottinghamshire County Council and www.picturethepast.org.uk.

Thank you to Creswell Crags Visitor Centre for supplying the overhead photo.

Picture of Eakring Oilwell in the 1940s – Courtesy of Doug Wallis.

Picture of Bison on Lascaux Cave wall – Courtesy of Semitour Perigord.

INTRODUCTION

Nottingham Castle, Southwell Minster, Wollaton Hall, Newstead Abbey and Newark Castle are places you would expect to see in any list of Nottinghamshire's main historical sites. But what about Laxton, Eakring Oilwell, Stapleford Cross, Stoke Field and Notintone Place – what part do they play in Nottinghamshire's history?

This book picks out a number of well-known, less well-known and obscure sites, each of which has a story to tell. The stories help to reveal some of Nottinghamshire's past and also allow a glimpse into British history. For example, the chapter on Eakring Oilwell tells the exciting tale of a British discovery that helped this country play a major part in winning the Second World War. At Stoke Field there is a headstone dedicated to 7,000 dead, mostly foreigners, victims of a battle which was to decide whether or not an impostor would take over as the next King of England. This chapter tells the story and explains why. The chapter on Trent Bridge cricket ground explains how the development of the game itself and its subsequent global impact makes this ground so special, not just to this county, but to the world.

This book doesn't just list all the known facts; visit the places yourself and pick up a small leaflet or guidebook and read the display boards on site – you will then have access to as many or as few facts as you wish. Nor is this book a list of all the historical sites in Nottinghamshire. Other sites have been left out due to space constraints, so you may not agree with the selection. Good! It shows you are thinking about it. Our past is worth all the thought you give it. It is our heritage, and the fascinating stories behind Nottinghamshire's role in British history are a great way to experience it. Forty sites have been listed in alphabetical order, with a short section at the end mentioning some of the sites that didn't quite make the main list.

Nottinghamshire Emerges

The Romans successfully invaded Britain in AD 43 and for nearly 400 years ruled and organised much of the land. After they left, in the early fifth century, our islands were invaded by Angles, Saxons and Jutes. They would have taken over existing settlements, by force if necessary, or created new ones. Over time, groups of villages became part of separate regions under their own King, and the various Anglo-Saxon kingdoms emerged, including Wessex (West Saxons), Mercia (from 'Mearc', meaning border people), Northumbria (Angles occupying the land north of the Humber) and East Anglia.

These kingdoms developed sub-districts so the King could organise his territory and levy taxes. In Wessex, a hide was the unit of land needed to support a family. Ten such units were called tithings and ten tithings were known as hundreds (a hundred families or hides). Groups of hundreds became known as scirs (Saxon for a piece shorn off, i.e. part of the King's land).

These later became known as shires and the King's representative, the scir reeve, became the sheriff. The earliest shire to be mentioned in documents was Hampshire in AD 757.

Shires appeared first in southern England. Some smaller areas kept the name of their kingdom – Essex (East Saxons), Sussex (South Saxons), Middlesex (Middle Saxons), Norfolk and Suffolk (both ancient divisions of East Anglia). Some shires took their name from the chief town, for example Hampshire (from Southampton) and Somerset (from Somerton). In middle and northern England, many shires took this route, for example Nottinghamshire, Derbyshire, Lincolnshire and Leicestershire, but only after England began to develop as a nation.

Viking Attack

Vikings had been raiding the country since the 790s. In AD 865 they landed in East Anglia with a great raiding army intent on plunder and settlement. By AD 870 they had taken over Northumbria, East Anglia and part of Mercia – only Wessex remained free of them. Alfred, King of Wessex, used the shire system to organise his kingdom into a unified defence against

Anglo-Saxon England, *c.* 870–880.

the Vikings. He needed to. During the 870s the Vikings strengthened their control, took over more of Mercia and began an assault on Wessex.

Alfred's kingdom was in dire trouble. He fought, and although things did not all go his way, he stemmed the Danes' advance. Finally in AD 878 he faced the Danish Army, led by Guthrum, in a crucial battle at Edington. In the words of Alfred's biographer, Bishop Asser, 'he attacked the whole pagan army, fighting ferociously in dense order, and by divine will eventually won the victory, made great slaughter among them, and pursued them to their fortress'. Alfred forced the Danes to retreat from Wessex, but, in view of the strength of the Vikings, signed a treaty creating a partition of Anglo-Saxon England. Eventually the part ruled by the Danes became known as the Danelaw and included the Five Boroughs of Lincoln, Stamford, Nottingham, Leicester and Derby, which the Danes were using as military garrisons and trading centres.

Following his victory at Edington, Alfred and his ally, Aethelred of Mercia, gradually took over parts of the Danelaw. In AD 899 Alfred died, arguably the greatest King to have ruled in Western Europe since Charlemagne. King Alfred's powerful successors, Edward and Athelstan, continued this re-conquest until they controlled most of the country. The Kingdom of England had emerged. Within this area the shire system became dominant. In many cases the word shire was just added to the name of the most important fortified town. Nottinghamshire was born as part of the process by which the Danish settlers of East Anglia and the East Midlands were absorbed into England.

Nottinghamshire didn't come first. The name Nottingham did, or more precisely, Snotengaham (a Saxon name meaning the village of Snot's people). Although not mentioned in the *Anglo-Saxon Chronicle* until AD 867, the settlement would have been established much earlier. Snot could either have been in one of the first waves of Angles who colonised many parts of the mainland, including the Trent Valley, or a leader of the settlement sometime afterwards.

Finally, after their victory in the Battle of Hastings, the Normans took over. They kept the shire system, although they began to refer to the shires using the French term – counties.

In 1087, Nottinghamshire had its own section in the Domesday Book, the comprehensive survey of the land compiled by William the Conqueror.

The shires remain one of the most ancient units of local government to have survived anywhere in the western world.

ARKWRIGHT BUILDING

The Robin Hood Regiment presented arms as a carriage and four brought the Duke and Duchess of Albany to the opening ceremony in 1881. The Gothic-styled building commissioned by the municipal corporation was the first college of higher education in England to be built financed from public funds. It was also the first building specifically for university use in the county. Four years before, former Prime Minister William Gladstone was present when the first stone was laid and commented 'at some distant date, perhaps, you may be speaking not of a university college, but of a University of Nottingham'. The college based at the Arkwright Building eventually evolved into that university, but also became a part of Nottingham's Trent University. The Arkwright Building is a symbol of an age when the availability of adult education was being spread ever wider. Like the Midland Station, it was built to impress.

A Changing Scene

In the nineteenth century, industrial processes were becoming ever more complex. The early lead of the British in manufacturing was being eroded by Germany, partly because they had in place a good system of technological education. There was a need for a place where mechanics and artisans could go to study the principles and theories of their trade. When Professor George Birkbeck ran a series of free lectures in Glasgow, hundreds turned up and the first Mechanics Institute was set up shortly after in 1821. Twenty years later there were 300 institutes, in which women were free to participate. Mansfield, Newark and Nottingham joined the ranks in 1831, 1836 and 1837 respectively. By the 1860s, Nottingham offered courses of lectures (mostly with voluntary teachers), a library, a museum and an art gallery all under one roof. In 1834 a School of Design opened in Heathcote Street aimed at Nottingham's growing textile industry.

The Arkwright building, 1881. (Courtesy of Picture the Past, NTGM011313)

Three in One

In 1866 James Stuart, newly graduated from Cambridge, began to lecture to working men in the northern industrial towns such as Leeds and Rochdale. His success led to Cambridge being asked to provide university teaching to other towns on a permanent basis. In 1873 Nottingham became the first centre in the country where an officially organised extension class was held and 1,832 people attended the first session. The need was there. Two other Nottingham businessmen began to discuss providing a building where lectures could be based permanently. At this time, Nottingham's Free Library and Natural History Museum were housed in temporary accommodation following a fire which destroyed the Mechanics Institute building in 1867. Why not combine all three?

An anonymous donor put up £10,000 to help fund the idea and eventually Nottingham Corporation found itself agreeing to provide the land on Shakespeare Street and to build premises to house a university college, library and museum. The Arkwright Building was born and it was a ground-breaking development. The corporation had provided funds at a time when it was more usual for private benefactors to foot the bill (as in Manchester where cotton magnate, John Owens, provided the funds for a new technical college in 1851, which eventually evolved into three separate universities of Manchester, Leeds and Liverpool in 1904). It was, however, a private individual who had started the process, and another one – Jesse Boot – completed the job in grand style.

Two Universities

When the Shakespeare site became too cramped, Jesse Boot became Nottingham's premier philanthropist. In 1919 he gave £50,000 towards establishing an East Midlands University. Two years later he donated the forty-nine acres to be developed into University Park, and a further £120,000 to enable building to commence. In 1922 the foundation stone was laid for the new University of Nottingham, and it was opened six years later.

Large parts of the Arkwright Building were destroyed during a bombing raid in 1941. Restored after the war, it became the Nottingham Regional College of Technology and later merged with the Nottingham College of Art and Design (the one that had begun life in 1834). This evolved into Trent Polytechnic and finally, in 1992, to Trent University.

Universities

According to the *Guinness Book of World Records*, the first degree-granting institution was the University of Alkaraovine, Fez, Morocco, in AD 859. Next came Cairo (AD 975), then Bologna (1088), Paris (1150), Oxford (1167), Cambridge (1209) and Salamanca (1218). By the end of the fifteenth century, another thirty-six had been added. As the nineteenth century dawned, England still had just Oxford and Cambridge, both serving the needs of the Anglican aristocracy and gentry. Scotland, however, had four – St Andrews, Glasgow, Edinburgh and Aberdeen – which were far more open, attracting able students from England and elsewhere. For university education to spread in England, the institutions had to open up to people of all religions, including Dissenters, Catholics, Jews and agnostics. University College London led the way, doing just that in 1828. In 1836 it became the University of London, England's fourth, as Durham had been established in 1832.

University education extended to the masses in the early twentieth century. From twenty-two universities and university colleges in the UK in 1918, the number increased to forty-four by the end of the 1960s and over 100 by the 1990s. As the student population rose, better facilities were constantly needed. The impressive, art deco Newton Building, designed by one of Nottingham's most prolific architects, Thomas Howitt, was erected to serve the Technology College. Completed in 1958, it was Grade II listed in 1998. A few years later plans were drawn up to restructure both the Newton and Arkwright Buildings. The plans involved demolishing large parts of the latter, invoking the wrath of various heritage groups. The Victorian Society managed to get the building listed as a Grade II and secured many improvements from the original scheme.

Viewing

The £70 million scheme is due to be completed in 2010. It will be part of the university campus, so ask if you can have a look around.

BESTWOOD WINDING HOUSE

Bestwood Winding House, one of Nottinghamshire's last remaining monuments to its coal mining history, still stands, despite the pit closing in 1967. It contains an enormous vertical winding engine, complete with cylinders, winding drum and brakes, and is unique in being the only such engine housed in its original building in the country. Yet it was nearly scrapped, only saved by a last minute preservation order. It then lay forgotten and neglected until, in 1985, a dedicated group of twenty ex-miners overhauled the moving parts and re-roofed the Grade II listed building. In 2007, the group received good news – £1 million National Lottery funding. Plans include a specially-designed glass lift to take visitors up the tower and a visitor centre with education facilities to be housed in a nearby derelict sub-station.

Bestwood Winding Station.

King Coal

Coal was a key factor in Britain's nineteenth-century economic supremacy and pits in this county played their part. At first the easily accessible coal was mined. In 1774, around fourteen pits between Eastwood and Wollaton (including Bilborough, Brinsley and Strelley) quarried coal from shallow pits where the seams met the surface. After they had been fully mined they left great depressions in the landscape, known as 'bell pits' (depressions still exist in the fields south of Strelley Broad Oak). The mining companies next followed the coal seams as they ran eastwards and deeper underground. To reach these concealed coalfields they had to sink pit shafts, and technological development (e.g. steam engines to pump out water, raise the coal and lower the miners and pit ponies) enabled this to happen throughout the country. By 1913, there were over 2,500 British mines producing 290 million tons of coal, of which 30 per cent was exported.

Coal mining was very labour intensive. In 1913, less than 10 per cent was cut by machine and between 1913 and 1927 the industry averaged over 1 million employed. Towns and whole counties were dominated by coal miners and the areas and estates which grew to house them. What happened at Bestwood Colliery (established 1872) helps us understand the crucial role of coal in the development of this country and its infrastructure.

A large industrial complex developed around the Bestwood mine, including an ironworks (Bestwood's four iron blast-furnaces were part of the fourteen within the county producing 205 tons of iron in 1907). It had its own railway yard with connections to the main line, as did all the local pits (Bestwood had its own station until 1936). Rail trucks rattled and clanged as they loaded and unloaded and carried the coal around the country. Spoil tips grew and 'often suffered from partial combustion and at night the effect created was dramatic, giving places like Bestwood and Hucknall a surreal atmosphere as the glow from these high-up fires lit up the sky for miles around'. (From *The Leen Valley At Work* by Martin Weiss.)

Sixty-four colliery houses were constructed in 1876, followed by a school, general office, church and institute. More houses followed and the colliery village grew. Planned colliery settlements were also established in Eastwood, Annesley, Pleasley, Forest Town, Shireoaks, Rainworth and New Clipstone. And Nottinghamshire still had plenty of coal. After the Second World War, the county led the way in mechanisation, including underground transportation and extraction systems. Large, brand new pits were sunk at Calverton, Beavercotes and Cotgrave, and vast modern housing estates were built to accommodate the workers.

During the twentieth century, oil became the dominant energy source. The motor car depended on it and other industries converted to it. Although new markets emerged in the form of the power stations, the use of coal declined so that by 1984 the workforce was less than 190,000. In that year the miners took on the government in a dispute over the future of the mining communities and 'who ruled the country'. The miners lost. Of the 170 working collieries in Britain in 1984, just twelve were still operating twenty years later. In Nottinghamshire, just Welbeck, Harworth (under threat) and Thoresby (a beneficiary of a recent £200 million deal to supply Cottam and West Burton Power Stations) remain. Of the pits that closed, many sites have been completely cleared (with spoil heaps re-shaped and planted), while others have been re-used as industrial estates. While most of the housing estates remain, the pit winding gear and associated industrial buildings have virtually all disappeared. Hence the importance of Bestwood.

The winding house is situated just inside Bestwood's 690-acre Country Park and open 364 days of the year. There is no visitor centre yet, just toilets, free car parking and miles of footpaths with some of the best bird watching in the county. In the village, Park Row is an excellent example of former colliery housing, complete with the stone company crest BCIC. The former company offices building also still exists – look for the tall clock tower.

BLYTH PRIORY CHURCH (ST MARY AND ST MARTIN)

You have to search for Saxon remains among the churches of England. Traces of Norman work, however, are commonplace. Within Nottinghamshire about 100 parish churches have Norman fragments within their structure. To find a decent-sized example is a lot more difficult. This county has the wonderful nave of Southwell Minster and the priory churches of Worksop and Blyth. For the latter two we have to be thankful they were also used as parish churches and hence were not completely destroyed during Henry VIII's Dissolution of the Monasteries. Much of Blyth's original structure has disappeared but the nave and the north aisle remain very much as they were in 1088 and are amongst the earliest examples in the country, alongside Ely (1083), Malvern (1084) and Gloucester (1090). Let me quote A.C. Wood. Blyth, Worksop and Southwell are 'all complete examples of the Norman style, and in them, with plan, form and detail before our eyes... we can catch something of the higher impulses which brooded over 12th century England'.

Reward the Soul
Blyth was built as a priory for Benedictine monks in 1088 by Roger de Builli. Builli was one of the Norman barons who threw in his lot with William, Duke of Normandy, and crossed the Channel in 1066 to challenge King Harold for the Kingdom of England. It was a risky enterprise and William promised to divide up the country amongst his supporters, once he'd taken it. This promise of a reward, combined with the very real threat of death if they lost, helped William secure a narrow victory. William kept his promise (he wouldn't have remained King for long if he hadn't), and Builli received land in Yorkshire, Derbyshire and Nottinghamshire. He quickly erected a wooden castle, just over the border at Tickhill in Yorkshire. Once the Normans had beaten off the various English uprisings they settled down and began to build in stone. As well as castles and churches, they also built monasteries.

Roger de Builli and his wife, Muriel, provided the money and the rights to taxes from various villages and manors to fund it. This was normal; by showing devotion to God, they hoped he would look after their souls. Besides, the impressive structure also played another role – it showed the locals that Builli was powerful and not to be trifled with.

Aliens
Blyth became a Benedictine priory (Builli's monastic order in Normandy) staffed originally by monks from the mother house in Rouen. To make ends meet, monasteries farmed the land or leased parts of it for others to farm. This, together with taxes from local churches and estates attached to them, was their main source of income. Some monasteries, including

Blyth, in turn passed on a portion of these rents and taxes to their parent house in France. This parent house would also appoint the prior and have the authority to recall him. Because of this, monasteries such as Blyth came to be known as aliens – an apt name. They were under foreign control, had many foreign staff and sent money overseas (just like certain foreign-owned businesses today).

Problems arose when England was at war with France. Could the alien monasteries be trusted and was it right for them to be sending money to the enemy? During King John's battles with France in the early thirteenth century, he ordered them to pay their taxes to the English Treasury. In 1295, Edward I seized all the alien priories, numbering about 100, and used their revenues to help pay for the war. Although lands were restored to the monasteries later, this seizing of their assets occurred regularly when war broke out. Finally, in 1414, all remaining alien houses were forced to pay their revenues to the King. In many cases their property was transferred to other monasteries.

Doom

In the early 1400s it was decided to separate the eastern part of the church, used by the monks, from the west and southern part, used as the parish church. A large wall was built and covered by a painting depicting God on Judgement Day directing the dead to Heaven or Hell. Doom paintings were a very powerful way of reminding medieval Christians that on Judgement Day their sins would be evaluated and they were to be consigned to either Heaven or Hell. Most worshippers could not read the Latin Bible nor understand the Latin the priest was using in his sermon. However, they could see the graphic pictures of the Devil, casting sinners into Hell's burning fires and the angels leading the saved up the ladder to Heaven. Situated at the front (chancel end) of the church, it was in full view as the priest took the service.

This splendid doom painting fell foul of Henry VIII's desire to marry Anne Boleyn. At the time, Henry was married to Catherine of Aragon, who had borne him six children, of which only one, a girl, had survived. The Pope refused to grant him a divorce. In defiant mood, Henry married Anne anyway in 1533 and was excommunicated. The next year he passed the Act of Supremacy, making him the Supreme Head of the Church of England. He was demonstrating that he could do what he wanted. Using his new powers, he began to confiscate the land and property owned by the monasteries. Around 850 monasteries were destroyed, Blyth being one of them.

Luckily, the large part of Blyth's church used by the parishioners was not attacked, except that, in a puritanical effort to destroy idolatry, the attackers whitewashed the wall painting. 400 years later part of the painting was rediscovered. In 1985, it was finally cleaned up. The whitewash had not destroyed the painting, it had preserved it! It is still there to see, the only such wall painting in the county.

Meanwhile on the monastic land to the east a hall was erected. In the 1680s the Mellish family, the new owners, knocked this hall down and erected an imposing, new, brick hall. This remained in their family until 1817 when it was sold to pay gambling debts. Finally, in the early twentieth century, it fell into decay, along with many such halls around the country, as owners struggled to pay death duties. It was demolished in 1973, leaving the splendid Norman church to take pride of place once again.

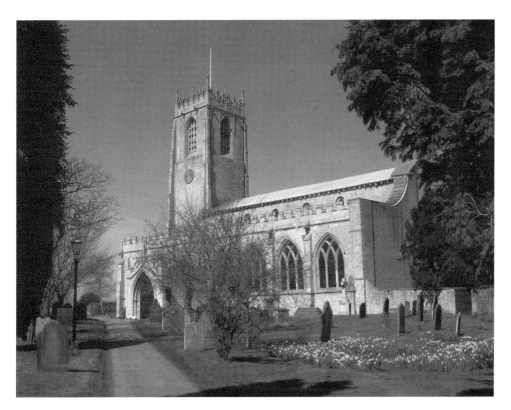

Blyth Priory Church.

Benedictines

The order was founded in the sixth century by St Benedict, son of a Roman noble, born around AD 480 in Nursia. He moved away from the temptations of the city and became a hermit, but his sincerity and character attracted followers. He set up twelve small monasteries, established schools for children and also built a large monastery at Monte Cassino. This was visited by many, including bishops and nobles, who were impressed by his principles of hard work, prayer and good deeds. He died around AD 545 but his influence lived on.

When St Augustine came to Britain in AD 597 on his mission to bring Christianity to the Anglo-Saxons, it was a Benedictine monastery that he established in Canterbury, the first outside Italy. Over the centuries monasteries based on Benedict's principles were founded across Europe, and amongst their famous members were the Venerable Bede of Jarrow, Alcuin of York and William of Malmesbury. Between 1529 and 1872, the Benedictines produced forty Popes. St Benedict's monastic organisation was also copied by the others – a cloister around which a library, chapter house, dormitory, refectory, kitchen, cellar, infirmary etc. were placed to enable an efficient daily monastic regime.

Visiting

Visitors must respect that this is a working church. Call the church warden to arrange a visit on 01909 591876. Leaflets are available. Ask if you can visit the tower.

Jesse is the name which springs to mind when thinking about Boots, but we must go back a generation to discover the roots of the business. Jesse's father, John, opened a small shop selling herbal remedies at 6 Goose Gate, Hockley, in 1849. John was brought up in a Methodist family. His mother, Mary, took an active part in the local community, running a school and administering herbs and potions to the sick. Between her and his religion, he was infused with a strong work ethic.

John died in 1860 and Mary took over the running of the store, aided by ten-year-old Jesse. In 1871, aged twenty-one, Jesse was made a partner of 'Mary and Jesse Boot, Herbalists'. Six years later he took over control, and in 1883 obtained a lease on a much larger shop, 16-20 Goose Gate, Boots second store. Before moving in he engaged a local architect to design it for his needs. Its most innovative feature was a two-storey shop front with large sheets of glass divided by elegant iron columns. The window frontage enabled him to draw attention to his shop and advertise his wares. By the turn of the century he owned more than 250 shops, the largest retail chain in the country. In 1933 Boots 1,000th store was opened in Galashiels, Scotland. In July 2006, the Boots Group Plc merged with Alliance Unichem Plc to create an international pharmacy-led health and beauty group, with over 3,000 retail outlets in twelve countries, employing over 68,000 people.

16-20 Goose Gate.

Jesse Boot was a remarkable man. In the early years, while other chemists kept prices up and concentrated on selling to the more well-off, Jesse kept his prices low. By selling more he was able to buy his materials in bulk, keep his costs low and make a profit. He treated his staff well, organising outings, a welfare officer and a newsletter.

In 1908 he contributed substantial funds towards the rebuilding of the Albert Hall and built the Dorothy Boot Almshouses for Army veterans. After the war he made a big donation towards Nottingham's General Hospital. In 1920 he provided thirty-six acres of land on the Victoria Embankment for a park and playing fields for the public and local schools, for which he received the Freedom of the City. In 1921 he helped Nottingham Corporation buy Woodthorpe Grange, and the forty-acre estate became a valuable public amenity. In the 1920s he poured money into developing the future Nottingham University at Highfields, including an ornamental lake, gardens, recreation grounds and a swimming pool.

Boots second store, with its elegant iron columns, is still there but is a Boots no longer. However, it was the first store Jesse chose, where he experimented with his retail format before exporting it around the country and, eventually, the world. Many people can start a store and run it well, but it takes a man of extraordinary resourcefulness and energy to create a successful, long-lasting retail empire. This site started Jesse on the road to wealth and influence at a time, before the Welfare State, when the sick and poor depended on charity and mutual support to survive, and when society expected the wealthy to contribute to philanthropic purposes. They did, and Jesse was one of the best.

Enlightened Entrepreneurs

Jesse wasn't alone. There arose in Britain in the nineteenth century a certain type of person who came from modest origins, built up business empires and used their profits for the benefit of the community.

Robert Owen (1771-1858) led the way. The son of an ironmonger, he married the daughter of the owner of a large cotton-spinning mill in New Lanark, Scotland. He bought out the business and ran it according to his principle that if you produce the right environment, then you produce good and humane people. He provided good housing, schools, free healthcare and subsidized stores for his workforce and banned physical punishment. Other manufacturers in his day could not see the profit in this expenditure, but his mills were very successful and became a showpiece for visitors from all over the world. His ideas received much publicity. Today the site has World Heritage status and the mill is a hotel.

George Cadbury (1839-1922) and Joseph Rowntree (1836-1925) both started out working in their fathers' small factories, introduced innovations that led to their concerns becoming household names and then created model villages for their employees. George Palmer (1818-97) expanded Huntley & Palmer's biscuit empire by introducing machinery until he was able to donate sixty-three acres to the people of Reading for use as recreation grounds and sports pitches. Thomas Holloway (1800-83) had much in common with Jesse Boot. Both spotted the opportunities for medicines that could be bought over the counter. In the nineteenth century the few qualified doctors that existed charged fees that were too high for the common man (often three times their weekly pay). By an aggressive use of advertising, Holloway built up an empire, manufacturing and selling proprietary drugs. In his sixties he became a generous philanthropist, founding the Royal Holloway College for Girls and the Holloway Sanatorium.

Others who built up substantial businesses and contributed to society's good included William Lever (Lever Brothers), W.H. Smith, Thomas Cook and Thomas Beecham.

Liberal Nonconformists

Most of these men were Nonconformists. Palmer, Cadbury and Rowntree were Quakers; Lever and Beecham were Congregationalists; Boot and Smith were Methodists and Cook was a Baptist. The argument that 'certain values stressed by Protestant Nonconformist groups contributed to the early rise of industrialisation in Britain', is constantly debated by economic historians and there is much to be said for it. These groups certainly stressed hard work, self-help, temperance and the need to contribute to the community, but there is also another side. From the late seventeenth century, Nonconformists were excluded from holding civil or military office and prevented from obtaining degrees from Oxford or Cambridge. Quakers, with their pacifist beliefs, were thus ruled out of an Army career. With artistic occupations seen as frivolous, many opted to make their mark in the world of commerce or industry.

Another common trait was membership of the Liberal Party, which campaigned to end the constraints on Nonconformists. After 1828, Nonconformists were allowed to become Members of Parliament, and many did so. Jesse did not, although he was President of the Nottingham Liberal Association from 1910 to 1931.

Pelham Street Store, opened in 1892 and designed to impress. It still does!

More than Herbs

In 1891 Jesse had an opportunity to show his hometown just how far he had come. He had already opened new stores in other towns, but now was ready to expand into general retailing. He acquired a new Nottingham branch near to the elegant shops of the town centre, in Pelham Street, and fitted it out in grand style. Helped by the artistic flair of his new wife, Florence (who helped him introduce books, stationery, etc.) he introduced entire departments for toiletries, perfumes and fancy goods. This store was remodelled in 1903 by local architect Albert Bromley and became the standard for future stores. The exterior design can be seen today, although this shop also is no longer a Boots. It is round the corner from the Goose Gate store and well worth a visit.

Visiting

These buildings are best viewed when visiting the Lace Market. These are working stores, not attractions.

CHESTERFIELD CANAL

The gates that take the Chesterfield Canal into the River Trent at West Stockwith are wide enough to allow river boats to enter. Opened in 1777, it was the first canal built in Nottinghamshire and one of the earlier English canals, completed before canal mania fully took hold. It is the best link to the Transport Revolution in the county. The canal made history by having the longest tunnel in the country at that time, 2,880yds long. When the tunnel opened in 1775, three boats carried 300 people through on an hour's trip as a band played to celebrate the occasion.

Before the canal, most of Chesterfield's trade travelled by packhorse along the road to Bawtry, thence along the River Idle to Stockwith. Here the cargoes of coal, lead, limestone, millstones, etc. transferred to boats, which followed the Trent to the east coast ports. The boats would return with sugar, tobacco, oils, wine and iron-ore etc. When news of the success of the Bridgewater Canal (1761) spread around the country, businessmen saw an opportunity. Josiah Wedgewood was a typical investor, supporting the ambitious Grand Trunk Canal linking the Mersey and the Trent. He realised it would be ideal for transporting both the heavy clay needed by his pottery factory and his fragile, finished pottery to the markets of the fast-growing towns. Completed in 1776, it was one of a number of canals that would provide a transport system for the country, enabling it to experience an industrial revolution before any other country in the world. By 1820, England had over 2,200 miles of canals.

In 1681 the 149-mile Canal du Midi was completed. It joined the Atlantic and the Mediterranean, and, by doing so, cut weeks off the travel time, enabling ships to avoid the pirates who lurked in the seas off the southern coast of Spain. Complete with 103 locks and the world's first canal tunnel, it was regarded throughout Europe as a tremendous engineering feat. In 1753, young Francis Egerton (Duke of Bridgewater) visited the canal while on a Grand Tour of Europe and was impressed. On his Worsley estates he had an abundance of coal, which was desperately needed by the large Manchester market. Unfortunately, transportation via packhorse and riverboat was expensive. By 1761 he had built a canal to link the coal and the city, including an 'impossible' aqueduct over the River Irwell. It was a huge gamble, but it paid off, halving the cost of coal in Manchester, and earning him and his engineer, James Brindley, both money and praise.

Canal gates at Stockwith.

Parliament gave assent to plans for the Chesterfield Canal on 28 March 1771 and the £100,000 capital needed was raised by July. It continued to be reasonably prosperous until the middle of the nineteenth century. The local Anston stone, used to construct the Houses of Parliament, gave the canal good business. Shipments started in 1840 and by the time they had been completed, approximately 250,000 tons had been despatched.

Narrow Boats

James Brindley was the engineer behind many of the early canals. He knew that to keep costs down, the locks would have to be restricted to a certain size. His locks were 72ft in length and 7ft 6in wide. Many canals followed this pattern but, being built by individual companies, variations occurred. Most were wide enough to allow for two boats to pass each other, but some were narrow with passing places. Boats therefore had to be long and narrow. They were also restricted to carrying approximately thirty tons, so they could be drawn by a single horse. This was still ten times more than it was possible to carry by a horse and cart.

Some canals were built extra-wide to allow riverboats to enter and use them. Various local shareholders in Retford agreed to provide extra funds so that the section of the Chesterfield Canal between Retford and Stockwith could take wide-beam boats straight from the River Trent.

Fall and Rise Again

Turnpike roads and canals were crucial to the Industrial Revolution, but during the nineteenth century railways took over most of the carrying trade. By the 1850s canal traffic had fallen by two-thirds. Some canals were bought out and closed down by railway companies, others soldiered on at much reduced profits. The early twentieth century saw many canals abandoned.

The Inland Waterways Association began to campaign for the restoration of the canal network in 1946, and several hundred miles have been restored. There are now fifty canal societies and trusts dedicated to preservation, and over seventy restoration projects being considered in England alone. Chesterfield Canal Society (formed 1976) aimed to fully restore the canal (unused commercially since 1908). It has been very successful in making most of the canal navigable. Now a trust, it faces the daunting task of bringing the 2,880yd Norwood Tunnel (collapsed in 1907) and the Thorpe Salvin staircase of locks back into the system.

Timeline

- Pre-700 BC – According to Herodotus, writing in the fifth century BC, the Grand Canal from the Nile to the Red Sea had existed for at least 200 years.

- 486 BC – The Chinese Grand Canal (over 800 miles) was completed, according to Confucius.

- 1488 – First recorded use of a pound lock (with gates enabling a boat to be raised or lowered to another level) on the Brenta Canal, Padua, Italy.

- 1566 – The Exeter Canal was the first canal in England to use pound locks.

The wide section of canal to Retford.

- 1642 – The Briare Canal connected the Rivers Loire and Seine, including forty-two locks.

- 1681 – Canal du Midi completed, connecting the Atlantic and Mediterranean.

- 1761 – The Bridgewater Canal opens, Britain's first true canal of the Industrial Era.

Other Local Canals

- The Erewash Canal (1779), connecting Langley Mill to the River Trent, gave the Derbyshire coalfields direct access to the hinterland of the river. Abandoned 1962.

- The Nottingham Canal (1796) carried coal from Langley Mill to Trent Bridge, and hence to Nottingham. Abandoned 1937.

- The Grantham Canal (1797) was 33 miles long, built to gain access to the coal carried by the Nottingham Canal. Abandoned 1936.

All now provide good walking.

Visiting

The Cuckoo Way (old towpath) is now accessible to walkers throughout its 43-mile length. The Chesterfield Canal Trust at Tapton Lock Visitor Centre, Chesterfield (01246 551035), has leaflets showing circular routes involving the canal. They also arrange boat trips from Chesterfield or Retford (01246 280660). Retford's Bay Tree Restaurant/Café, an eighteenth-century warehouse, serves refreshments by the canal. You can walk from here to the aqueduct over the River Idle or hire a canal boat from West Stockwith (01522 514774).

CRESWELL CRAGS

Around 50,000 years ago the limestone gorge known as Creswell Crags wasn't surrounded by trees as it is today. It was covered by grassland upon which mammoth, reindeer, wild horses and bison grazed while keeping a wary eye out for lions, wolves, hyenas and other predators. Neanderthal man was also on the lookout for prey, but he used spears and traps. Over the next 40,000 years, the climate warmed and cooled and the ice sheets advanced and retreated. During one of the warmer periods, 30,000 years ago, *Homo sapiens* (modern man) first made his appearance here. In the last warmer period, 13,000 years ago, which we are still experiencing today, modern humans returned and some of them left their marks on the cave walls in the form of animal drawings. The story of their discovery gives us an insight into history itself.

We now know that the first human apes appeared in Africa 4 million years ago, but, in the early nineteenth century, the starting date for most people for the beginning of the world was around 4000 BC (based on the book of Genesis).

Aerial view of Creswell Crags.

In 1816 Christian Thomsen was appointed head of the Antiquarian Section at (what later became) the National Museum of Denmark in Copenhagen. He decided to arrange his ancient objects by the substances they were composed of. The terms Stone Age, Bronze Age and Iron Age were born. This was the first attempt to put pre-history into some sort of order and it helped people understand the stages of development of our species into modern man. In the 1860s people began to read Darwin's notion that man had evolved over thousands or millions of years, and Lyall's idea that Earth's physical features too had evolved over millions of years. The true depth of man's history began to be realised, and the search was on to discover the earliest evidence of humankind's origins. In 1864, in some of the rock shelters of the Dordogne region of France, a piece of mammoth ivory was discovered with a carving of a mammoth on it, conclusive proof that man had lived in the remote past alongside creatures long extinct.

More people joined the search. One such was the Revd Magens Mello, a keen geologist and local historian. In 1875-76 he began the excavation of some of the caves of Creswell Crags and discovered an abundance of ancient animal bones alongside Stone Age human tools.

Cave Art

During the late nineteenth century, discoveries were made of drawings and paintings on cave walls, but claims that they were Palaeolithic (early Stone Age – before 10,000 BC) were dismissed. However, in 1895, some startling evidence was discovered in a previously unknown cave at La Mouthe in the Dordogne region of France. In order to reach the previously undisturbed cave, excavators had to remove material of Palaeolithic origin. The drawings behind had to be of the same age! Once the authenticity of cave art had been proved, other discoveries followed because people knew what to look for.

Bison back-to-back on the Lascaux Cave wall. (Courtesy of Semitour Perigord)

In 1940 a spectacular find of 600 paintings and nearly 1,500 engravings was made at the Lascaux cave in the Dordogne by two teenage boys. The paintings, possibly the best in the world, date from around 17,000 years ago and, interestingly, one wall still has the sockets that held the beams used by the artists for scaffolding. Finds have since been made in many countries, including Spain, Italy, Russia, the Americas and Africa dating between 10,000 to 30,000 years ago.

No discoveries, however, were made in Britain. Was it due to a thick layer of ice covering much of Northern Europe at this time? In 2003 a team of scholars examined the cave sites known to have had Stone Age deposits but had not been subject to thick ice – Creswell Crags (Nottinghamshire/Derbyshire border), Paviland (Wales), Kent's Cavern (Cornwall) and Gough's Cave (Cheddar). They made an amazing discovery at Creswell of more than eighty engravings on the caves' ceilings and walls of animals including bison and several different bird species – the only known examples of Palaeolithic cave art in Britain. Why hadn't they been seen before? The archaeological team, led by Professor Paul Bahn, were working in April and May and were able to see the caves illuminated by clear, brilliant sunlight. They were also looking for evidence of cave art, whereas Mello wasn't.

The Oldest Sites in Britain

Neanderthals' teeth have been discovered at a site in Pontnewyd in Wales, dated to around 200,000 BC. Remains from 500,000 BC, indicating evidence of hominid occupation, have been found at Boxgrove in Sussex and in East Anglia, current excavations are showing evidence of hominids from 700,000 BC. So Creswell wasn't the first or only home for the Neanderthals in Britain, but it is an impressive site. Church Hole Cave, penetrating 60 metres into the rock, has more than eighty engravings on its walls and was occupied intermittently until Roman times. Pin Hole Cave was a prehistoric hyena den and was also occupied by Neanderthals. Among the finds include a bone engraved with a human figure.

Visiting

At Creswell you will discover a country walk, an excellent visitor centre (with a good, inexpensive guidebook) and thousands of years of prehistory. Admission is free but charges are made for the Ice Age, Rock Art and Cave and Collection Tours. For opening times and availability contact the centre on 01909 720378 or visit www.info@creswell-crags.org.uk.

D.H. LAWRENCE'S BIRTHPLACE

Coal made Eastwood. In the early 1800s it was a small settlement of around 100 people. 100 years later it was a coal mining town with a population of over 4,000. Arthur Lawrence grew up in this community and worked underground at Brinsley Pit. He spoke with a broad local accent, liked a drink or two and could just about read the local newspaper. In 1875 he married Lydia Beardsall, a reasonably well-educated girl with lower middle-class parents. She liked to write poetry, had assisted a teacher in a local school for a while and grown up with strong Nonconformist ideas, including abstaining from drink. Their marriage produced one of England's best-known writers, D.H. Lawrence.

The house of his birth dates from 1845 and was one of a great many erected to serve the needs of the coal miners and their families. As the industry ran down during the mid-twentieth

Beauvale Board School. D.H. Lawrence attended from 1893-98.

century, many were demolished to make way for more modern homes. Luckily the Borough Council had enough foresight to intervene to save ninety-two of them in this area. They still retain their quaint brick outbuildings and small, fenced gardens, and have been renovated externally to their original condition, although the roads are now tree-studded walkways.

The house is now the D.H. Lawrence Heritage Centre, where you can experience a miner's home and see much Lawrence memorabilia. Leaflets direct you to the various Lawrence Trails and the landscape that inspired him. Within easy walking distance are the four family homes that trace their gradual rise up the social ladder. Mrs Lawrence was the force behind this rise, seeking a way out of the close working class trappings in which her husband was enmeshed. After experiencing the tensions within his parents' marriage, Lawrence wrote stories concerning the joys and the sorrows that exist in the personal relationships of husbands and wives, and parents and children.

Not far from the house is the former headquarters of the local pit owners, Barber Walker & Co. where Bert Lawrence, as he was known throughout his childhood, would pick up his father's wages. It is now the Durban House Heritage Centre, where you can delve more into both a miner's life and Lawrence's. It also has a restaurant and art exhibition. As a visitor you feel wanted, but its future is uncertain due to a funding review. However, it is the role that Lawrence's novels played in shaping society's attitude to sexuality and censorship that propels both him and this site into the limelight.

Censorship

D.H. Lawrence was a prodigious writer, producing thirteen novels, nearly 1,000 poems, plays, travel books, some non-fiction and some rather good paintings. Several of his books are regarded as works of genius by many in the literary world, but it is for one book that he is best known. Lawrence experienced problems over censorship from the start of his writing career, so by the time *Lady Chatterley's Lover* was ready, publishers were more than wary. They knew the book could fall foul of the 1857 Obscenity Act whereby books could be seized if they had a tendency to deprave and corrupt, even via a single passage. They refused to touch it, so in 1928 he chose a small Florentine bookseller to print 1,000 copies privately. These quickly sold out via his circle of friends, but publishing privately meant he was unable to establish copyright, so pirated versions soon appeared. He refused to authorise any of them and instead issued further editions, which again sold out.

The fame of the book spread amongst the English-speaking world. In 1930 a bookseller in America, where obscenity laws were similar to Britain's, was sentenced to four months in prison for selling a copy, adjudged obscene literature. It was banned in Canada and shortly after in England. From 1932 to 1943, many different printings of expurgated versions found their way onto the market in an attempt to satisfy the public's curiosity. In 1944 a court case ruled there was reasonable doubt as to the obscenity of the novel, yet the book remained banned.

In 1954 the Obscenity Act was revised. The new version had four main tenets:

- No conviction if publication is in the interest of science, literature, arts or learning.

- Opinion of experts may be admitted.

- Authors may speak in defence.

- The work is to be read as a whole.

In 1958, Grove Publishing printed 30,000 copies in the USA and stood to lose a lot of money if they could not be distributed. Despite an outcry from the religious community, Judge Bryan declared it was 'an honest and sincere novel of literary merit'. Distribution was allowed. The gates were open. In 1960 Penguin Books attempted to publish in England and were prosecuted under the new Obscene Publications Act. It was to be a test of the new law. After a lengthy trial, during which many high profile witnesses defended the book, they were acquitted. A precedent had been set. People scrambled to buy the paperback that had caused so much trouble. A new age of liberality of censorship had been entered. It was far too late for Lawrence though. He had died in 1930.

Outsider

In 1912 Lawrence met Frieda von Richthofen, the wife of Nottingham professor Ernest Weekly. They fell in love and she left her husband and three children for him. During the First World War, Lawrence and his wife were unable to obtain passports and were targets of constant harassment from the authorities. Frieda's cousin was the German pilot, Baron Manfred von Richthofen (the 'Red Baron' said to be responsible for the shooting down of Captain Albert Ball, Nottingham's very own air ace). They were accused of spying for the Germans and officially expelled from Cornwall in 1917. In 1919 they were allowed to emigrate and their wandering began. They lived in various countries around the world, including France, Switzerland, Italy, Austria, Australia, Ceylon and the USA.

For local people, for much of the twentieth century, even his name was unwelcome. Doors were slammed on researcher Enid Goodband when she sought local opinion. He based many of his characters on local people, depicting them in an unfavourable light, especially his own father. Opinions differ as to how much Bert disliked his father, but most locals found it natural to identify with the man who worked hard all his life and went to the pub with his mates, rather than his intellectual son known worldwide for a book banned for being too sexually explicit.

Visiting
D.H. Lawrence Birthplace Museum and Durban House (01773 717353). Also visit the local library, the large section containing his books and biographies shows, more than anything, that most people now accept him here.

EAKRING OILWELL

In August 1942, Britain faced an oil crisis. U-boats and bombing raids had destroyed much of the country's reserves, and Rommel's army was disrupting supplies from the Middle East. Oil was desperately needed to continue the war and before the Allies could even think to attack the European mainland. At an emergency meeting in London of the Oil Control Board, Philip Southwell, a representative from D'Arcy Oil, told the delegates about the potential of Britain's own oilfields. Most of the listeners were astounded. British oilfields! What oilfields?

Up until that time only a few people knew of the discoveries of oil in the Eakring area during 1939 and 1940. The search for oil in Britain had begun during the First World War.

Eakring Oilwell in the 1940s.

As submarines threatened supplies, the government set out on a serious search for oil, but not until the end of the war, in 1919, was a significant find made in Hardstaft, Derbyshire.

Who owned the rights to the oil? The 1934 Petroleum Production Act solved the problem by declaring Crown ownership of all oil not discovered up to that date. Prospectors applied for licences to explore and sunk exploratory wells throughout the country. At Eakring, tests revealed very high quality oil in sufficient quantity to make it the centre of the first commercial UK oilfield.

Following Southwell's revelation, it was decided to develop the East Midlands oilfields as quickly as possible. The first thing they needed was new and better drilling equipment, and the place to get it was America. Southwell was sent over straight away. In early September, in Washington, he met American oilman Lloyd Noble. Noble, heavily committed to other projects, turned him down. Southwell was desperate and hitchhiked a ride on a British Naval plane to New Orleans, from where he transferred to Oklahoma. He asked for directions to Lloyd Noble's home and turned up to plead with him again. They talked. They had both been to college and both served in the First World War. They got on, and Southwell got his drilling rigs. What the Americans were to call 'the English Project' was up and running.

Before the end of 1942, forty-four American oil workers arrived along with specialist equipment. In a year they sank 106 wells, pulling out over 3,000 barrels a day (at forty gallons to the barrel). By the end of the war, Dukes Wood and Eakring oilfields had produced over 2.2 million barrels, equivalent to around forty-three full, sea-going tankers – almost the same total as the number of tankers lost to the enemy.

Churchill's Greatest Secret

Churchill knew that it was crucial to keep the operation a secret. This was not an easy task when, during the peak production year of 1943, around 1,200 workers travelled to the site daily. Also, the Americans attracted attention. They caused a stir when they wore their Stetsons and cowboy boots on a visit to Newark, but told the locals they were making a movie. Most people in the area did not know what was going on, but those that did knew to keep quiet.

After the war the expertise gained by Eakring's oilmen was crucial to the development of the North Sea oilfields. Most of the drilling engineers had trained there, and many of the drilling techniques were first developed and tried there. The drilling section of the rig used to make the first hydrocarbon discovery in the British sector in the North Sea was pre-assembled at Eakring.

Further onshore fields were discovered at Egmanton, Bothamsall and South Leverton in Nottinghamshire and other sites in Lincolnshire, Leicestershire and Dorset, all initially run from Eakring. Oil is still being produced at Gainsborough today.

From D'Arcy to BP

The D'Arcy Oil Co. began when two brothers struck gold while prospecting in Australia in 1882. In 1901 they obtained an exploration licence in Iran and struck oil in 1908. The company grew and became BP in 1949, but lost its Iran operations in 1950 when the Iranian oil industry was nationalised. The subsequent return of experienced oilmen to Britain helped the domestic industry.

Visiting

The land comprising Dukes Wood Oilfield and Museum is about 2 miles south of the village of Eakring, and was donated to Nottinghamshire Wildlife Trust by BP in 1989. On the nature trail you can see butterflies, wild orchids and nightingales, but you will also see some of the 'nodding donkey' pumps that helped this and the other English oilfields produce 47 million barrels of oil up to the 1960s – all before any field in the North Sea had even been drilled. One of the aims of the small museum is to demonstrate just how important oil production, both onshore and offshore, has been to this country since 1942. Near the museum is a statue in honour of the forty-four Americans. One died when he fell off a rig and is the only civilian buried in the US Military Cemetery in Cambridge. Eakring's site acts as a lovely setting to an inspiring story.

The reserve is open at all times but the small museum (situated in an old hut) run by volunteers is not, so check before you go (01623 883332) or (01623 882446). A twenty-minute film is available on request.

THE GREAT NORTH ROAD

All roads lead to Bawtry! Not a statement that trips lightly off many tongues, yet three prominent Nottinghamshire roads did just that for hundreds of years:

- Littleborough to Bawtry Roman road.

- Medieval North Road, through either Mansfield or Ollerton, to Bawtry.

- The third way emerged in the thirteenth century. Crossing the Trent via Newark Bridge, the Great North Road (GNR) also passed through Bawtry. It became the main route north, and the Littleborough ferry declined in use.

Most travellers on these roads were not actually headed for the town, they were trying to avoid something else. Bawtry was the most easterly point at which roads could cross the River Idle and avoid the swamps of the far north of the county.

Bawtry is in Yorkshire, but only just. It was the destination for both Raedwald, King of East Anglia, and Aethelfrith, King of Northumbria, in AD 617. They came to do battle near the bridge over the River Idle. Raedwald won and became the premier King in England. It is most likely his grave that was discovered at Sutton Hoo.

The old road can still be followed physically, but it can also take you through the story of turnpikes and coaching inns (so well illustrated by Retford) that played such a vital part in the Transport Revolution.

Turnpikes
In the seventeenth century the roads were dire – hard, dusty and pitted with deep rucks in summer and sticky quagmires in winter. As trade and letter post increased (the Inland Postal Service started in 1635), requiring more travel, the government had to act. They allowed private companies to obtain an Act of Parliament to improve a section of road and charge a toll for its upkeep. Turnpikes were born. The first Act was passed in 1663 and by 1830, 4,450 Acts had been passed. In 1750 it took ten days to travel from London to Edinburgh; by 1830 it took just two. By 1836, over 3,000 coaches were in use and coaching inns sprang up all over the country.

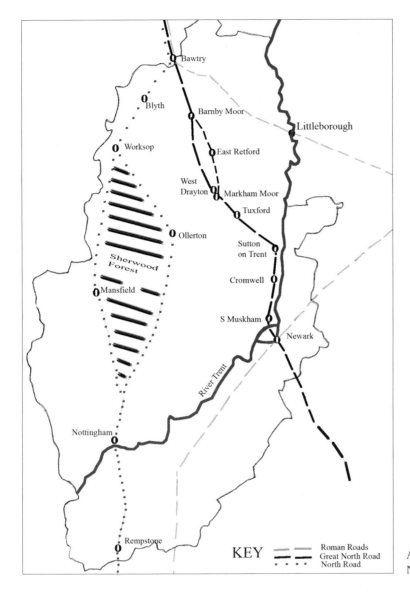

KEY ⟨legend⟩
- Roman Roads
- Great North Road
- North Road

A map of the Great North Road.

Some acquired good reputations, such as the Bell at Barnby Moor in Nottinghamshire. By the middle of the eighteenth century it had stabling for 120 horses and plenty of accommodation.

The first turnpike in Nottinghamshire (1725) covered the GNR from Grantham to West Drayton. Forty years later the whole of the GNR had been turnpiked except for the section between Markham Moor and Doncaster. Retford had an opportunity. Prior to the 1760s, the GNR had bypassed the town, bearing left at Markham Moor and meeting the Retford/Blyth road at Barnby Moor (Landranger OS Map 120). Travellers would use the coaching inns of Tuxford, the Jockey House on the bypass or those of Barnby Moor; Retford was out of the way. If it could improve its roads before the bypass was improved then the town would have access to all the road travellers and their business. The 1766 Act did just that, adding Retford to the GNR's itinerary.

Above: Newark Turnpike, 1813. (Courtesy of Picture the Past, NCCE003336)

Left: Retford Square, 1910s. (Courtesy of Picture the Past, NCCN000930)

A turnpike tollhouse still stands near Littleborough as a monument to this era. It is the octagonal-shaped house opposite Thornhill Lane. Most tollhouses were demolished in road-widening schemes.

Retford

Following the diversion of the GNR through the town, the people of Retford celebrated (until this time, the River Idle had been the main trade route). A few years later came the Chesterfield Canal, passing south of the square across the River Idle aqueduct. The church bells tolled for four days – more business was on its way. Trade and population gradually increased. The White Hart experienced rapid expansion and by 1828 had nineteen scheduled coaching services a day to London, Edinburgh, Newcastle, Nottingham, etc. The town became prosperous enough to have its own theatre in 1789. In this Georgian period many new houses were erected which still survive today in the square, Carolgate and Grove Street.

Fall and Rise Again

The road system and its network of inns were hit very hard by the coming of the canals and railways. But after the First World War, the rise of the motor car led to a renaissance of the GNR. Roads were widened, bridges replaced level crossings and some villages were bypassed. By the 1950s the GNR was an amalgam of ancient, Roman and medieval roads and modern highways stretching between London and Edinburgh. Renamed the A1, it was gradually brought up-to-date. Amongst the changes, the main road from Newark to the North was re-routed via Blyth (albeit bypassed), leaving the Retford to Bawtry section of the GNR to become the A638. To deal with the volume of traffic, many minor roads were cut out and petrol stations replaced coaching inns. But the number of cars on the roads multiplied and the A1 couldn't cope with the new level of traffic on its own, so a brand new road, the M1, emerged to ferry cars through the county. And this one missed out Bawtry from the start.

Books

'The Great North Road', a nineteen-page booklet by F.W. West (former Archdeacon of Newark) relates a vivid picture of both the road and its times. Try to buy it, but there is a copy in the Local Studies Library.

Visiting

It is still possible to follow the route of the old road by car for much of the way through the county. A good itinerary is the A616/B6325 Newark to Cromwell (using 1 mile of the A1). Then take the B1164 via Sutton-on-Trent, Weston, Tuxford, West Markham, and West Drayton to Elkesley while pondering that this was the premier road to Scotland and the North in the 1950s. Or take West's advice and walk the section between Jockey House and Barnby Moor on the pre-1766 Old North Road.

It is also rewarding to visit the many old coaching inns along the road. Some are much changed, but many still have an archway through to the area where the stables had been. Newark has some good examples – the White Hart (part fourteenth century), the Clinton Arms (formerly the Talbot, as known by Byron), the Saracens Head and the Castle Inn (resting place of William Cobbett, author of *Rural Rides*). See also the Newcastle Arms (in Tuxford, formerly the Crown), the White Hart (in Retford), the Swan (Bawtry) and the Scrooby Top (in Scrooby, now a restaurant).

GREEN'S MILL, SNIENTON

In 1400, around 10,000 windmills were in daily use in England providing the power to grind wheat and corn into flour. The website www.windmillworld.com lists over 1,000 mill sites in England, although many are disused, derelict or converted to other uses. The ongoing website www.nationalmillsweekend.co.uk lists around 120 English windmills, with opening hours. (A booklet listing around 450 wind and watermills open to the public either regularly or occasionally – 'Mills Open' – is available at £5.50. Details on site, or contact 020 7456 0909). Nottinghamshire has three such windmills listed, including Green's Mill. This mill ceased production in the 1860s, was restored in the 1980s and officially re-opened in 1985. It is a splendid sight, making it easy to understand why so many people are interested in the old mills today.

Green's Mill.

In 1972 Professor Lawrie Challis heard rumours that Green's Mill was about to be demolished and created a fund for its restoration. It attracted enough donations from around the world to buy the mill and donate it to the city. Much of the money raised, however, was not as a result of it being a mill, but of it being the place where a certain Mr George Green lived and worked for a while.

George Green

George Green was a mathematical genius who developed a general theory of potential, from which the theories of electricity (underlying twentieth-century industry) were derived. His theories were so advanced they were not understood by his contemporaries and were only rediscovered and fully appreciated after his death.

He was only eight years old when he spent four terms at Robert Goodacre's school in 1801, the best and most expensive school in Nottingham. That was his schooling! He left to work in his father's bakery business. In 1807 his father bought some land and built a windmill in which George was to work for many years. There he had a relationship with Jane Smith, the daughter of the windmill's manager, with whom he had seven children. However, his relationship with mathematics was possibly even stronger.

Where did he obtain his knowledge? In 1823 he joined the Nottingham Subscription Library, established in Bromley House in 1816. It gave him access to the Transactions of the Royal Society of London, in which Green could read the latest mathematical work published here and in other countries. The library still exists on Angel Row, and was one of a number of independent libraries set up in the late eighteenth and early nineteenth centuries for the general public to further their knowledge. George Green's success is a prime example of how influential they could be in an age well before the advent of publicly-funded, free libraries. Another possible influence was John Toplis, a one-time near neighbour and headmaster of Nottingham Free Grammer School, who was very interested in the new French mathematics.

Green published his main theory in 1828 while working full time at the mill. He was finally persuaded to study at Cambridge University in 1833 and produced several important papers before his death in 1840. In 1846, Green's work was rediscovered by Lord Kelvin, who popularised it for future mathematicians. The theoretical physicist, Julian Schwinger, used Green's functions in his ground-breaking work on quantum electrodynamics, for which he was awarded the Nobel Prize in Physics in 1965.

Much more can be learnt about this extraordinary man and his work at Green's Mill.

Timeline

- 400 BC – A reference to windmills in a Hindu book indicates their use at this time.

- Eighth century AD – The principle of the windmill was brought to Spain and Portugal by the Arabs after the Moslem conquest. For much of Europe, energy was supplied by human and animal muscle power, harnessed to simple ploughs and corn-grinding stones to make the bread, animal feed and ground barley for beer. The flat bread, similar to a ciabatta today, would often be a week or more old when it was eaten, as few bakers would have baked on a daily basis. However, as population increased, more bread was needed and the first step forward was the use of water power.

- 1086 – The Domesday Book recorded 5,624 watermills throughout England, virtually one for every village. However, streams were not reliable, drying up during the summer drought. So, as improvements such as gearing and horizontal shafts led to an increased power output, more windmills were installed. The earliest were of the Post type, in which the miller had to turn the whole mill to face the wind. In later types, the Smock and the Tower mills, only the top of the mill, the cap, rotated to turn the attached sails into the wind.

Some Local Mills

- North Leverton Windmill. A tower mill, in working order, built in 1813 by a syndicate of local farmers. Small admission charge (01427 880573).

- Ollerton Watermill. See separate chapter.

- Tuxford Windmill. A fully working, four-sailed, tower mill. Small fee (01777 871202).

- Greens Mill, Snienton. Easily accessible by bus from the city centre, both the mill and the adjacent science/visitor centre, where refreshments and books are available, are free to enter (0115 9156878).

KING'S MILL VIADUCT

Firsts

The nineteenth century saw the introduction of steam trains in England and their spread throughout the world. A claim to be the first railway or railway viaduct is therefore important, especially so in a country whose heritage is becoming increasingly valued.

Nottinghamshire lays claim to the distinction of having had England's first railway system. In the early 1600s, rails were laid at Willoughby's coal mines in Wollaton to transport the coal to a ready market. The rails were made of wood and the wagons pulled by horses. 100 years later things hadn't moved on a great deal technology-wise but wooden railways were becoming commonplace in some coal mining areas. In 1767 iron rails were introduced. By the 1820s iron rails were in general use but most carriages were still horse-drawn. The early history of railways cannot be said to have been revolutionary.

Causey Arch (1725), a 103ft single-arched structure crossing Tanfield Moor in County Durham, lays claim to be the world's oldest surviving railway bridge. In 2002, television's *Time Team* attempted to find the world's oldest multi-arched railway bridge viaduct. They identified Blaenafon in South Wales – built in 1790 to carry coal to the ironworks. The site was unfortunately covered by industrial waste and impossible to excavate. Machine Bridge, Pontypridd, built in 1809 to carry coal from the Rhondda Valley to the Glamorganshire Canal is, however, still standing. With three arches it has a good claim but faces competition from Laigh Milton Viaduct on the Kilmarnock-Troon Railway. Built in 1812 by William Jessop, who had built the Cromford Canal, it has a respectable four spans and has recently been skilfully restored. Jessop's son, Josiah, was asked by the owners of the Mansfield-Pinxton Railway to construct King's Mill Viaduct. He completed it in 1819 and, with eight arches, it can claim to be the earliest railway viaduct still standing in England.

King's Mill was there at the beginning. It is an important link with Nottinghamshire's industrial stirrings and allows us to tell the railway story.

Don't Miss Out Mansfield

The demand for coal for metal working, for soap boiling, for sugar refining, for brick-kilns, for domestic use and for the early steam engines was so great that anyone who could get the stuff to the towns and factories more cheaply would make a lot of money. This profit motive led to the development of canals in the early eighteenth century. The Chesterfield Canal supplied coal to Worksop and Retford, while the Erewash and Nottingham Canals moved coal from the west Notts' coalfields to Nottingham and Newark via the River Trent. Their success brought down the cost so that people and businesses wanted even more.

By the end of the eighteenth century, Mansfield still had no direct access to coal other than by turnpike road, yet demand, especially from the brewing industry, was great. At last, in 1813, local businessmen made plans. Despite opposition, the Mansfield-Pinxton line became the first railway in the East Midlands to be incorporated by Act of Parliament (1817). The track was eight miles long and horses or bullocks pulled the trucks to the summit at Kirkby, where they were set free to roll down the reverse incline to the canal wharves at Pinxton (the lock basin and canal pub have been restored and make an attractive site). The first load of coal arrived in Mansfield on 13 April 1819, and an excited crowd watched as coal was ceremoniously burnt in the marketplace.

King's Mill Viaduct.

Steam Locomotion

The introduction of steam engines to run on iron-rails was a massive milestone within the Transport Revolution. Richard Trevithick built the first locomotive to run on rails in 1804 and exhibited his invention at the London Exhibition in 1808. This set more wheels turning – those in people's minds. William Hedley built the Puffing Billy for use on the Tyneside Colliery railway lines and soon after, in 1814, George Stephenson introduced his first engine. Progress may appear slow but, as well as the engines themselves, the tools and the expertise to make them had to be developed too. By the mid-1820s Stephenson had developed an engine good enough to be used regularly for pulling coal-trucks on the newly built Stockton to Darlington railway. Built to carry coal, it opened in 1825 with a steam locomotive hauling trucks full of passengers along its 26-mile length, making it the first passenger railway. It continued to carry passengers, but, as steam engines were unreliable, horses were the main source of power.

However, Stephenson's success led to him being appointed chief engineer to the proposed Liverpool to Manchester Public Railway in 1826. This railway, designed to carry coal, cotton and corn, was also intended for passengers from the start. In 1829 the directors set up the Rainhill Trial to assess whether steam locomotives could pull passenger trains and to select the best engine. There were five entries and Stephenson's Rocket won, having achieved the heady speed of 30mph. The line opened in 1831 – the first purpose-built passenger railway in the world. It was such a success there was a rush to build railways everywhere. By 1843 there were 1,952 miles of railway open in Britain, by 1848 about 5,000 miles and by 1855 nearly 8,000 miles.

Competition

In July 1832 the Leicester & Swannington Railway opened, allowing Leicester direct access to its own coalfields. The very next month the Notts coalfield owners met at the Sun Inn, Eastwood, to plan an extension of the Mansfield-Pinxton line to Leicester in order to compete. This project eventually developed into the Midland Counties Railway, and in 1839 the Nottingham to Derby section of the line opened, finally bringing passenger services to Nottingham. In 1849, as the company smoothed out the curves in the lines, the King's Mill Viaduct was bypassed.

Bennerley Viaduct.

Other sites

Nottinghamshire's railways had many viaducts, including Bulwell (420yds long with twenty-six arches, now demolished), and Bennerley (near Ilkeston, Grade II listed, one of the last remaining wrought iron lattice-girder bridges in the country). Also, Mansfield town's nineteenth-century viaduct has fifteen arches, making it one of the largest in an English town.

Viewing

The site is always open. Park at King's Mill Lake Visitor Centre where there are refreshments and some literature.

LACE MARKET

In 1897 Nottingham became a city. It should have been named Lace City. 40,000 people, a third of the city's 1907 working population, earned their living from lace and its ancillary trades – dyers, bobbin makers, machine manufacturers, designers, draughtsmen, carriers and such like.

Houses needed fashionable lace curtains, tablecloths and bedspreads. Women's clothing (bodices, sleeves and skirts) had to have yards of lace edging. The Lace Market firms sent representatives with their pattern books all around the world to collect the large orders that this bustling place thrived on. It didn't bustle through lace making – that took place in workshops and factories in the suburbs. The Lace Market was aptly named; it was where the lace was finished, stored and marketed, but not where it was made.

In 1913-14 there were over 200 firms finishing and marketing lace, most with offices in the Lace Market. Today the area has trendy bars, restaurants and boutiques, but most of the large buildings have been converted to offices and flats. Roger Watson Laces of Western Street is one of the few survivors. Yet most of the grand buildings have survived. Anyone with imagination can still wander back through time to the days when horse-drawn carts trundled back and forth with 'lace in the brown' (unfinished) and finished lace destined for the export markets via canals, trains and ships. If you timed your visit to coincide with the dinner hour, you'd even be lucky enough to see hordes of ladies streaming from the finishing factories.

Beginnings

It started with William Lee's Stocking Frame in 1589 (see Ruddington's Framework Knitting Museum). This was gradually adapted to produce lace good enough to be embroidered by hand and marketed as 'Nottingham Lace' by the end of the eighteenth century. In 1808 John Heathcoat introduced the Bobbinet machine, which twisted the threads, producing lace very similar to the handmade version. Five years later John Leavers brought out his lace-manufacturing machine, still famous and in use today. Both machines produced quality lace in a fraction of the time required by the hand knitters. When these machines were harnessed to steam power in the 1840s, production increased and prices fell, creating even more demand. In 1825 there were 953 Bobbinet machines in Nottinghamshire. By 1831 it is estimated that 5,000 machines were in use locally, and that around three-quarters of machine lace was being produced within a twenty-mile radius of Nottingham. Most of it was plain net, needing hand-embroidering. This required more workers, and these workers needed somewhere to live.

A Change of Use

Nottingham was surrounded by large, open fields owned and controlled by the burgesses, the more well-off citizens of the town. Enclosure would simplify ownership, allowing development for housing, but the burgesses resisted until the mid-nineteenth century. Instead, the rapidly rising population swelled the surrounding villages (see Lenton Priory). They also poured into Nottingham, whose population rose from 28,861 in 1801 to 57,407 in 1851. Back-to-back slums arose in the few areas where space was available. One such area was Woolpack Lane, on the edge of the old, Anglo-Saxon part of the town which, until the later part of the eighteenth century, was mainly residential and rural. Dominated by St Mary's Church, it was also home to schools, the Town Hall and many mansions with large gardens. However, as the workers moved in, so the gentry gradually moved out. This gave the wealthy lace and hosiery manufacturers an opportunity. They too were looking for space to build large, impressive warehouses where lace could be finished and shown off to the buyers. They bought the houses with their large gardens, knocked them down and soon converted the rural scene into a huge, industrial complex, many of the buildings being five-stories high.

A view of the Lace Market from St Mary's Church.

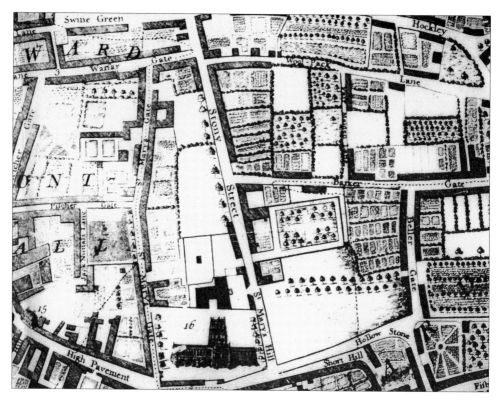

Badder and Peat's 1744 map of the Lace Market.

By the 1830s, fifty-eight manufacturers were located there. More quickly followed. Thomas Adams erected the E-shaped Adam's Building in the 1840s, possibly the finest Victorian lace warehouse to survive in Nottingham or anywhere in the country. It had six floors, eleven staircases, a library, a classroom, washing facilities, a workers' dining room and even a chapel. Plumptre House was purchased and demolished by Richard Birkin in 1853. He created a new road, Broadway, on which he built four large warehouses, including his own headquarters. By 1881 there were around 180 lace manufacturers in Nottingham, most being represented in the Lace Market. Buyers needed to go nowhere else.

Fickle Fashion

In 1841 the Jacquard system of punch cards was added to the Leavers machine, enabling the production of lace with a wide variety of patterns. In 1846, John Liversey adapted the Leavers machine to produce curtains. In 1839, the railway came to the town. Demand and production soared. But lace was part of the fashion industry. The First World War, as well as disrupting England's markets around the world, heralded new, unfussy styles not needing lace adornment. Lace was seen as old-fashioned. Demand fell and firms went bankrupt. Between 1910 and 1937, the number of lace firms in the Nottingham area declined from 220 to eighty-five, and buildings became redundant. By the 1950s and early '60s, some buildings had been demolished and the area was widely seen as in terminal decline.

Leeds, Bradford, Manchester and others with previously thriving textile industries also suffered as cheap imports flooded the markets worldwide. The question facing the city councils was should they demolish the unused Victorian buildings to make way for car parks, ring-roads, high-rise flats and offices? In the 1960s, Nottingham City Council planned to build Sheriffs Way, connecting Mansfield Road through the Lace Market with Maid Marion Way. It would have taken little heed of the city's history and heritage. Luckily for Nottingham, the Department for the Environment stepped in and rejected the plans, but not before Barker Gate was widened and areas on St Mary's Gate were flattened and used as temporary car parks.

Renovation

The late 1960s were a turning point. People began to see old buildings as architecturally significant.

The Civic Amenities Act (1967) allowed for the establishment of Conservation Areas and local authorities were encouraged to provide grants to restore buildings. 1969 saw Nottingham's first Conservation Area – the Lace Market. It was to be regenerated in several ways:

- For tourism, Shire Hall set up as a Museum of Justice. Also, the Lace Museum was established (since converted to the Pitcher & Piano public house).

- The retail area of Hockley was encouraged.

- Quality flats and apartments were supported.

- The Adams Building was developed into a further education college.

- Ice rink redeveloped into a new multi-use stadium. Broadway Cinema and Media Centre assisted.

The Lace Market was saved from the early 1960s modernisers, but how many people using it as a cultural area realise just how important the lace industry has been to Nottingham?

Two of Nottingham's major industries of the twentieth century were aided in their initial start up by the availability of skilled machine fitters, many of whom gained their skills working on lace machines. Raleigh Cycles, set up in 1890 after the early success of Humber Cycles (1868), was making 40,000 bikes per year by 1909. In 1877, John Player transformed a tobacco business and built three new factories on Radford Boulevard, soon to employ 7,000.

Viewing

See map on pp. 42-43. Hopefully the new square (completed 2008) with a special lace sculpture and a two-storey restaurant (as yet unoccupied) will become a new focus for the area. Perhaps in the future it will also be the home of a lace museum. For now, go to Ruddington's Framework Knitting Museum and Nottingham's Industrial Museum at Wollaton Hall to experience some of the machines, and read Sheila Mason's excellent book *Nottingham Lace 1760s-1950s* or *The Lace Market, Nottingham* by Geoffrey Oldfield.

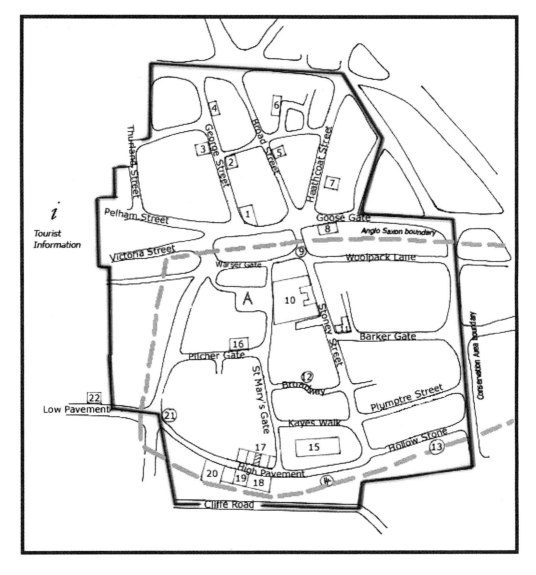

KEY TO LACE MARKET MAP

1   George Hotel. Now the Comfort Hotel. Only survivor of three hotels which served the buyers from around the world. The Flying Horse is now an arcade, and the Black Boy was demolished.

2   Cooperative Arts Theatre. Part of the regeneration after a Conservation Area was declared in 1969. The aim of the areas was to preserve the character of England, not just castles and cathedrals.

3   Watson Fothergill's office. He designed it and also many of Nottingham's famous buildings. His style was very distinctive, with intricate detail and complex, turreted roof-lines.

4   Early nineteenth-century house on Broad Street, with lace makers' workshop windows on the top floor.

5   Broadway Media Centre – also part of the regeneration. Began life as a Wesleyan Methodist chapel holding 2,500 people. In 1820, prior to industrialisation, the Lace Market had one church, eleven chapels, three Sunday schools and five hospitals. William Booth, the founder of the Salvation Army, was converted at this chapel.

6   Roger Watson Laces. One of the few survivors of the lace trade in the Lace Market, still doing what many used to do – buying lace, preparing it and selling it.

7   Nos 12-14 Heathcoat Street. Former residence of the Consulates of Spain and the Dominican Republic. As many as nine foreign consulates were once sited in this vital area for trade.

8   Jesse Boot's first big store. He chose this site to target the thousands of workers in the lace industry. His father's first, small, herbalist store was also on this street (No. 6, now demolished).

9   Stoney Street. In 1866, thirty-six lace manufacturers and agents shared buildings on this street. From the second half of the nineteenth century it would have been bustling with workers, mostly female, on their way to and from work and during the lunch break. Also horse-drawn carts would line the streets, delivering the lace made in the tenement factories of Radford, Basford, Beeston and elsewhere, for storing and finishing by the 'manufacturers'. After it had been dyed, cut and embellished to customer's requirements it was delivered around the world by cart, barge and train.

10   The splendid Adam's Building, designed by T.C. Hine. Hine designed many of the houses in The Park and many important churches and buildings around the country. Probably the largest and best lace warehouse to survive anywhere in the country, it even boasted a chapel where a chaplain conducted a service for the staff every morning at 8 a.m. Now it is a college of further education.

11   Lace warehouse designed by Watson Fothergill.

12   Broadway. New road created by Richard Birkin after purchasing and pulling down Plumptre House in 1853. It was designed deliberately with a curve in the middle to give the impression from both ends that it was a cul-de-sac and hence more exclusive. Birkin's former HQ is at No. 5, designed by T.C. Hine. Within the Birkin archway are two Norman windows separated by a beast's head, believed to have come from the Norman St Mary's Church.

13   Hollow Stone. For centuries this road, which turns south towards the Trent, was the main road south out of Nottingham.

14   Georgian town houses on High Pavement. In 1910 there were thirty-four references to lace manufacturing and lace agents for this address in one directory.

15   St Mary's Church. One of the best 'non-cathedrals' in the land. Its history can be traced back to before the Norman Conquest, and the first church on the site was possibly built by the early tenth century. This, the third building, was mostly completed by 1475. It is a splendid site with many links to Nottingham's history, and where you can try your hand at brass rubbing.

16   Milbie House, Pilcher Gate. It was built in 1889, designed by Watson Fothergill. The use of top designers indicates the importance lace merchants put on impressing their clients.

17   County Tavern (now Cock and Hoop), where merchants could hear the latest lace-trade gossip.

18   Shire Hall. From here the Sheriff ran the county and presided over the local shire court. Dates back to at least the fourteenth century, but the former timber-framed building was rebuilt in 1769 with Assizes and new prison facilities. The front was restyled by T.C. Hine in the nineteenth century. Now houses the very informative tourist attraction, the Galleries of Justice Museum.

19   Old County Police Station, complete with lamp.

20   Dissenters Chapel built in 1691 when 1,400 hearers met weekly. It was rebuilt in 1876 and became the Lace Centre in the 1990s, intending to cater for Lace Market tourists. Sadly it did not attract enough business and is now the Pitcher & Piano public house.

21   Copy of the original Weekday Cross, site of the daily market from Anglo-Saxon times until around 1800.

22   No. 13 Low Pavement, next to Lloyd's Bank, was the site of the US Consulate in 1893.

A   Constructed in 2007-08, this square is the new focus of the Lace Market with a two-storey restaurant and a special lace sculpture.

LAXTON

Laxton is not an impressive site to the eye, but it is unique. A thirteenth-century peasant returning for a nostalgic visit would still be able to recognise the village layout – the church (albeit much changed), the castle mound (sadly not the castle) and, most impressive of all, the field layout. Laxton's big claim to fame is in being the only village in the country to retain its medieval strip-farming system. The village even retains a legacy of medieval organisation. A Court Leet still meets every year in the Dovecote Inn with legal status to impose fines on anyone abusing manorial law. Its powers are not as strong as they were, but each year a jury is sworn in, entrusted with the task of ensuring the system is run fairly and that farmers have not encroached on another's strips or on common land. Laxton allows us an insight into medieval organisation and has a local pub serving up-to-date food with old-world service.

Laxton Church.

The Open Field System

The land of the village was divided into two or three fields. In the three-field system, one field was cultivated by winter crops (wheat or rye), another with spring crops (barley or oats), while the third was left fallow to recuperate. The fields were divided into strips, intermingled in every direction, with each strip representing a day's ploughing (usually an acre). The strips were open in the sense that they were not surrounded by hedges as most fields are today. Furthermore, they were generally cultivated in a communal way, the peasants working together to plough the strips in turn, although the produce went to the individual owner of that strip. The advantage of the communal system was that all the peasants could rely on their strips being ploughed by the others when they were called away on military service, as constantly happened during the Middle Ages. The peasants could also see if the others were pulling their weight.

The system evolved from around the ninth century onwards in much of Europe. During the tenth century, the population of Europe began to grow again after dropping to its lowest level since Roman times, following years of constant raids by Saracens, Magyars and Vikings. The increased population meant more land was needed for cultivation and much of it came from the woods and unused uplands surrounding the villages. The new land was shared amongst the peasants, each having a strip of the good land and the not-so-good; another advantage of the strip system.

Most peasants in the Middle Ages, apart from some freemen, were tied to their local lord of the manor, unable even to leave the manor without his permission. In return for the right to farm their land, they had to perform regular services for their lord without being paid, such as working a few days a week on his land or serving as his warriors. In his turn, the lord of the manor had to provide services for his local baron or earl, and, continuing upwards, these had to provide money or a quantity of armed men whenever the King demanded it. This system of payment-in-kind in return for land held was an essential part of the feudal system. On a local level each lord organised his own manor, so the system is referred to as the manorial system.

The Fall of the Open Field System

Increasingly during the twelfth and thirteenth centuries, the peasants converted the services they owed their lord into a money payment. To earn money to pay their dues, they would work harder on their own land to raise surplus produce, which they sold at the nearest town, or they worked on the lord's land in return for a money wage.

After the Black Death of 1348-49, during which over a third of the population perished, there was a chronic shortage of men to plough the fields, so the manorial lords often had to pay higher wages. This led to land being enclosed and put out for pasture. Keeping sheep required less labour and there was a constant demand for wool.

The disadvantages of the open field system were the cause of its decline. Not only was there much waste of land between the strips but, most important of all, the system was inflexible – all the landholders had to do the same things at the same time. If someone wanted to experiment with different crops at different times, they couldn't. Nor could anyone decide to enclose a piece of land with a hedge in order to rear more sheep; they first had to get the agreement of the owners of the majority of the land, and this entailed an Act of Parliament.

For the Industrial Revolution of the eighteenth and nineteenth centuries to occur, agricultural practices had to change. They did. There were two great periods of enclosure: during the sixteenth century when wages and the price of wool rose during a long period of inflation, and during the eighteenth and nineteenth centuries when the more wealthy landlords realised they could be even better-off if they controlled their own land. Between 1760 and 1815 3,289 Enclosure Acts were passed, and by 1850 nearly all of the agricultural land in England was enclosed. The pretty, parcelled-up, patchwork quilt land of England was born. It made possible more efficient farming, stock breeding which improved the quality of cattle, and better drainage and manuring. New crops, such as turnips, were introduced, providing winter food for cattle. Previously many cattle were slaughtered over winter because there was no feed for them. The improvements enabled agricultural production to keep pace with the demand from an increased population, a phenomenon that was both a cause and a result of the Industrial Revolution.

Laxton Survives
Only 25 per cent of the open field land of 1635 exists today, and the strips that remain have been enlarged to accommodate machinery. So enclosure crept up on this village too, but was prevented from taking over, firstly by a disagreement between the owners and then by one owner, Earl Manvers, being too involved in building Thoresby Hall to have funds available for enclosure.

Castle, Church and Village
To defend his newly-conquered land, William ordered castles to be built at key defensive sites. Three early motte-and-bailey castles were built at Nottingham, Tickhill (just inside the Derbyshire border) and Laxton. The owners' names clearly indicate the nature of William's takeover of the country – Roger De Busli (Tickhill), Geoffrey Alselin (Laxton), and William Peverel (Nottingham). This was mirrored throughout the country as the Domesday Book of 1086 lists the new French owners of the land. Laxton Castle was important from the twelfth to the fourteenth centuries when Laxton acted as an administration centre for Sherwood Forest. At that time barracks, an armoury, stabling, kitchens, domestic quarters, barns, granaries, forges, etc. would have been situated within its fortifications. The earthworks are the largest and best preserved in the county.

The village street is interesting, being lined with small farmsteads as well as houses and a church (1190s, but much remodelled and extended).

Visiting
The visitor centre (01777 871586) is open 'all day, every day'. Admission is free and a good booklet can be purchased with map and suggested walks. There is also a heritage museum (01777 870376).

LENTON PRIORY

'While the royal castle of Nottingham yet remained a construction of wood and earth, there arose, little more than a mile away and within view of the defenders of the castle, the Priory of Lenton, built in the massive stonework of the Norman style'. So wrote E.L. Guilford in his impressive book on Nottingham in 1857. There is very little left to see of Lenton Priory, which is a shame because in the Middle Ages it was not just the most important religious institution in the county, but also the tenth richest priory in England and well-known in Europe. The venue for the largest trade fair in the county for several centuries (more important than the Goose Fair), its story serves to illustrate several strands of the county's history.

How Big?

When the priory was built, Lenton was a small, open-field village. The priory church and ancillary buildings (dormitory, guest house, granary, bakehouse, kitchen, chapter house, cloisters, etc.) dominated the skyline like a small town. Possibly enclosed by a stone wall, its lands would have stretched from Old Lenton across the university, almost to Beeston. How big was the priory? According to excavations conducted by Herbert Green prior to 1936, the overall width of the nave and aisles, including the walls, was 80ft, or 140ft if we include the transepts (the short arms of the church). The comparable figures for the majestic cathedral at Southwell are 72ft and 135ft respectively.

Not only was the priory big, it was also far-flung. Founded somewhere between 1109 and 1114 by William Peverel, an early charter ensured it would be a growing concern by generously endowing it with land and property to bring in an ample rent. Among its endowments were seven mills; the townships of Lenton, Radford, Linby and Langar; the three Nottingham churches; the tithes (taxes) of Peverel's fisheries, lead works and venison rights in Derbyshire; part of the tithes of his demesne pastures in the Peak District, including Buxton, Stanton and Chelmorton; and the churches of Harlestone, Courtenhall, Irchester and Rushden in Northamptonshire and Foxton in Leicestershire, along with a few other bits!

Why Was It So Big?

The Normans converted to Christianity in the tenth century and had a plentiful supply of stone. New stone-built cathedrals, churches, monasteries and castles appeared all over Normandy in the eleventh century, and, after they had conquered England, they had a whole new land in which to show off their building skills. The mega-rich nowadays buy yachts, islands and soccer clubs, but then, to show off your wealth, you needed a castle, a cathedral or a monastery. And there was another attraction – the conquerors, who ruthlessly put down any rebellion against them, wanted to show their pious side. Even if the locals didn't buy the story, surely they themselves would have a better chance in the life-to-come if they had provided a glorious, new monastery for the community!

Lenton Priory as it is now!

Why Did It Become So Small?

After the Dissolution of the Monasteries in 1538, many were turned into farms or houses for the gentry, as at Newstead. Others, like Lenton, had all their stone and lead stripped from them so that there was virtually nothing left (Blyth and Worksop monastery churches survived because they were used regularly by the local congregation). Lenton's lands reverted to pasture until the rise in industrialism in the eighteenth and nineteenth centuries resulted in a demand for new houses. The Burgesses of Nottingham refused to allow the construction of houses and factories on the common lands surrounding the medieval limits of the town, so a ring of villages within reach of the town experienced a rapid rise in population. In 1768 the first Lenton and Radford Enclosure Award was granted, the open fields were destroyed and the site of Lenton Priory disappeared.

VILLAGE/YEAR	1801	1851	1901
Beeston	948	3,016	8,960
Radford	2,260	12,637	35,354
Basford	2,124	10,093	27,119
Snienton	558	8,440	23,093
Lenton	893	5,589	23,872

Lenton population, 1801-1901.

A Cluniac Monastery

Lenton was a member of the Cluniac Order, named after Cluny Abbey in Burgundy, founded in 910. Cluniac monasteries spread over many lands but were closely dependent upon the foundation abbey, to which they were obliged to pay tribute on a yearly basis. During periods of war between England and France, the King forbade the Cluniac priories from sending money abroad (see Blyth Priory). In 1392 the monks of Lenton Priory were formally naturalised so that their first obligation was to their country, not their order. The names of the Priors of Lenton reflect this change. Three of the last five were John Ilkeston, Thomas Nottingham and John Annesley, while before them came Peter de Sirimiaca, Astirgius de Gorciis and Peter de Abbeville. By the end of the fifteenth century, the Abbot of Cluny took very little interest in the English houses; they were Cluniac in name only.

Why Was Prior Heath Hanged?

By the beginning of the sixteenth century, monasteries had largely outlived their usefulness. According to Trevelyan's *History of England*, the life of the monks was one of 'easy sauntering comfort without grave offence but without marked benefits to the world around them'. When Henry VIII sent round his commissioners to gain information, they reported widespread immorality. However, it is now recognised that these reports were biased, the fate of the monasteries had been decided before they set out and they were there just to collect the 'evidence'. The monks who made their job easy by admitting to 'crimes' were rewarded, such as the Prior of Thurgaton who, after admitting adultery, received Fiskerton Hall. Prior Heath of Lenton admitted nothing, so he, two monks and four lay brothers were hung, drawn and quartered, probably in Cow Lane (now known as Clumber Street).

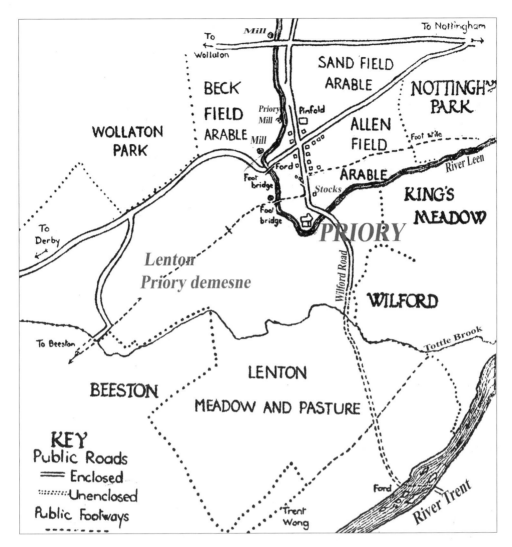

Map of the priory dominating Lenton.

Visiting

Parts of the old priory have survived, but you have to go looking for them. The last remaining pillar stump of the majestic church is on Priory Street in a small, railed enclosure. It makes for a sombre visit.

The most visible remain is the priory church, on the corner of Gregory Street and Old Church Street. This building, now mainly Victorian, incorporates a twelfth-century chancel. It once stood in the grounds of Lenton Priory and was probably the hospital, caring especially for those suffering from 'St Anthony's fire', a skin disease sweeping the country at that time. In 1538 the villagers transferred their parish into this church, along with the font from the destroyed priory church. This font is another survivor. 300 years later, in 1842, it was moved to the newly-built Holy Trinity Church on Church Street, New Lenton, a grand, dark-stoned, Victorian building which looks forbidding from the outside. Inside though, it is very welcoming, as is the font. It is nearly square, carved in the twelfth century, and one of the finest in the country. It is also still in regular use, as it has been for over 900 years. The Church of Holy Trinity and the priory church are both working churches. Best to use the website (www.lentonparish.org.uk) and send an email to book a visit. Some open days are being planned. Be sure to contribute to church funds.

Two other artefacts remain – some floor tiles, now in Nottingham Castle Museum, and a stained-glass window, now in Nuthall Church.

LITTLEBOROUGH TO BAWTRY ROMAN ROAD

Just north of Lincoln, a Roman road branched off from Ermine Street, heading towards Doncaster, York and the North. It crossed the Trent on an 18ft-wide stone causeway (removed in 1820 as a hindrance to navigation, but the stone base can still be seen when the water is very low) to enter Nottinghamshire at Littleborough. Here the Romans built a fort, Segelocum, to protect the river crossing. There are two references to this fort in the Antonine Itinerary (a second-century Roman guidebook). Finds here include coins, pottery, a Roman altar and, in 1860, a coffin, which revealed the body of a young woman whose cloak was clasped by a brooch. The body disintegrated within a few moments of the coffin being opened, but the coffin is in Lincoln Cathedral.

Littleborough to Bawtry Roman road.

So, the crossing is no more, but the road from Littleborough is. You can walk in Roman footsteps towards Bawtry in safety, as it is no longer a major road but a minor one, ambling along between some very pretty Nottinghamshire villages, home to interesting churches and cosy pubs. It would almost be a crime not to walk along this stretch of road which allows us a glimpse into Roman history.

Roman Remains

Is there much to see en-route? A pint or two at the local pubs might help, but this walk could easily take you back to the Roman era. Littleborough to Clayworth is the best section. Although it disappears for short stretches at Sturton-le-Steeple and South Wheatley, it runs straight all the way to Haughgate Hill, just past North Wheatley. For much of the way there are continuous ditches and wide verges beside the road, raised above the surrounding ground by about 2ft, typical of a Roman agger. From Haughgate Hill a change of direction enables the road to follow the higher ground towards Clayworth, where it meets the Chesterfield Canal. Past Clayworth, and next to the road, the canal enters Drakenholes Tunnel. During its construction, a lot of Roman material was unearthed.

Aggers

The Romans built their roads on raised embankments, aggers, enabling the road to drain naturally, and those using it to have a good view of the countryside around. Soil from the side of the road was used for the base, leaving a drainage ditch. Next was a layer of large stones, then several layers of smaller stones or gravel. The agger could sometimes be 4 or 5ft high.

Not all Roman roads were straight, although many were for long stretches, as their surveyors would use small hills to place a siting mark and run the road straight to the next mark. However, if an obstacle showed itself they would aim to miss it, but keep the next section straight. A map of Roman roads in Britain will show many long, straight sections with sudden changes of direction. Nottinghamshire's section of the Fosse Way is a good example, shifting direction near Cotgrave and East Stoke to allow for the Trent.

The Fosse Way is one of the longest Roman roads in the country (from Seaton on the south coast through Cirencester and Leicester to Lincoln). It is also Nottinghamshire's most important Roman road, with four identified Roman settlements. It enters the county at Willoughby, where the Roman town of Vernemetum stood. Travelling north, the road makes a sharp right turn on its way to Margidunum (sited on the large roundabout by East Bridgford). Here a 6½-acre site was once enclosed by timber walls, later changed to stone (possibly after Boudica's rebellion). Next on the route is the small town of Ad Pontem (East Stoke), and then finally the major settlement of Crococalana (Brough). However, there is now little to see, although much of it is raised above the surrounding land. Regular A46 users will know this road is notorious – keep your eyes on the traffic.

Conquest and Decline

There was a great deal of Roman settlement in both county and country, as evidenced through aerial reconnaissance. Over 250 settlements in the county have been identified from crop marks on aerial photographs, including the forts/camps of Calverton, Farnsfield, Edingley and Gleadthorpe. Also revealed is an extensive landscape of Roman fields, trackways and settlements in both North Nottinghamshire and South Yorkshire.

To Danum (Doncaster), York and the north

Ermine Street to York and the forts on Hadrian's Wall via the ferry over the Humber

Bawtry

● **Scaftworth**

● **Segelocum**
Littleborough

O (Retford)

Fossdyke

O (Tuxford)

● **Lindum**
Lincoln

(Mansfield) O

Fosse Way

Southwell Villa ●

● **Crococalana**
Brough

● **Newark**

River Trent

● **Ad Pontem**
East Stoke

Broxtowe Fort ●

(Nottingham) O

● **Holme**

● **Margidunum**
East Bridgford

● **Flawborough**
Ruddington

Ratcliffe On Trent ●

Site of Roman Temple.'

Coins, brooches and pottery held by Castle Museum but not on display

● **Vernemetum**
Willoughby

To Ratae (Leicester), Cirencester, Ilchester and Exeter

ROMAN NOTTINGHAMSHIRE

Over 250 settlements identified from aerial photographs, including 9 military installations and 12 probable villas. As well as the main roads there would have been a network of minor roads.

● Roman Site

Main Roman roads.

The forts along the Fosse Way were abandoned late in the first century AD, but remained as settlements. As the Roman Empire came under increasing pressure in the fourth century AD, Nottinghamshire came to the fore once again, becoming a border area between north and south. A fortlet was constructed at Scaftworth (near Bawtry) to defend the bridge over the River Idle, and the Fosse Way forts could well have been refortified.

A word of caution. Terry Jones, in his *Barbarians* (an alternative version of Roman history), reminds us that Celt-built wooden roads supported a European-wide trading network – the Upton Track in South Wales dates back to the fifth century BC. The Roman road system was unique for its construction methods and its extent – by the fourth century AD there were some 53,000 miles of road connecting Rome with its empire.

Medieval En Route

- Sturton-le-Steeple – church rebuilt around 1180 with fourteenth-century tower. Norman fragments built into the vestry wall.

- Clayworth (Clavord in the Domesday Book) – church has Norman doorway and thirteenth-century chancel arch.

- Everton – eleventh-century Norman church enlarged 1150-80 and restored in 1869.

According to Bede, writing in the early eighth century, Littleborough was the site where Paulinus, a monk sent by Augustine (the Pope's envoy to Britain), baptized a large number of people in the River Trent watched by Edwin, King of Northumbria. Edwin perished in AD 633 during a battle with Penda, the pagan King of Mercia. There is a legend that Edwin's body was taken to Edwinstowe's church, hence its name. When Penda died in battle in AD 655, Mercia reverted to Christianity. Littleborough's tiny church, possibly the smallest in use in England, has a fine Norman chancel arch. But we are on a Roman trail here, so concentrate instead on the Roman tiles used in the herring-bone masonry in the church walls.

Visiting
From Littleborough to the busy A631 (best avoided) the road is quiet. Nottingham University Archaeology Museum (0115 9514820) has a permanent display of items from Margidunum. To see the Roman material at the Castle Museum you will need to phone the History and Archaeology Team (0115 9153620) several weeks in advance.

MIDLAND STATION

Railways were born to carry heavy goods such as coal, iron and salt. People are heavy too, and in the 1820s the idea emerged to use trains to carry passengers. The first purpose-built passenger railway was opened in 1831 in England but, although this notion was copied throughout the world, the driving force for the spread of railways remained the ability to carry minerals such as gold and copper in Africa, nitrates and silver in South America and coal and tea in India. Passengers were an important afterthought!

Stations
Passengers required stations. Richards and MacKenzie, in their extremely informative and readable book *The Railway Station*, estimate that between 1830 and 1950 almost 140,000 stations

were built in the United States, around 2,000 in New Zealand and almost 200 on the small island of Sri Lanka. Station numbers in Britain reached 9,000 in the late nineteenth century as developers fell over themselves to build lines, but this was reduced to 6,000 by 1955 after many duplicated lines were closed down or amalgamated.

Nottingham started late, its first station on the Midland site being erected in 1839 to serve the newly-built railway line to Derby (its gate piers still remain at the entrance to the present Magistrates Court off Carrington Street). After the railway's success, new lines quickly followed, to Newark/Lincoln (1846) and Kirkby-in-Ashfield and Mansfield (1849). A functional, larger station was constructed on Station Street in 1848, but was soon outgrown. Finally, in 1904, the third and present station was built on the same site. Designed by A.E. Lambert while railways were at their peak of importance and over forty stations existed within an eight-mile radius of Nottingham, it was built with prestige in mind. It had to be at least as good as the impressive Great Central's Victoria Station, designed by Lambert only a few years before (now the site of the Vic Centre shopping complex, with only its ornate clock tower remaining). This Midland Station was built with red brick and terracotta, and is described as Edwardian Baroque (ornate and extravagant in style). It cost £1 million and, according to the *Evening Post*, was 'architecturally pleasing'.

Stations as Art

A European traveller in the eighteenth century would have been sure to visit the cathedrals on his route. They were the living illustration of the glorious age of stone building (between the eleventh and fourteenth centuries) that saw over eighty cathedrals and hundreds of large churches spring up throughout Europe as towns competed with each other to have the most splendid building. Such a traveller in the late nineteenth and early twentieth centuries would have found the latest results of civic rivalry right on his travel itinerary – the railway station. The essence of the nineteenth century, firstly in Britain then throughout Europe, was self-confidence and grandeur. As the population and wealth of the towns expanded, so industrialists erected prestige factories (e.g. in the Lace Market), towns erected new Town Halls and libraries, and, caught up in the excitement of the railway age, they also built splendid railway stations.

This spread of a new type of building throughout the world was amazing, but just as amazing was the diversity of styles. Richards and MacKenzie put it beautifully, writing 'one might have expected that imperial railway powers, marching masterfully across their colonial territories, might have laid down, at least within specific countries or along particular routes, a series of uniform stations, rather like the Roman's forts and marching camps.' But no, they used local building materials and local architects to fashion a whole multiplicity of styles. And yet certain trends have been identified. Carroll Meeks, in his influential book *The Railway Station*, identified four stages in the development of station architecture. The first was 'the emulation of one style', in which the early stations attempted to copy Greek and Roman styles, e.g. Huddersfield (1850) and Amsterdam's Willemspoort (1843). The next stage, the 'synthesis of many styles', took the form in England of the Italian villa style, as exemplified by Chester General (1848). From the 1860s to the 1890s there was 'the take-off to creativity' in which different styles were used to create fabulous stations in different countries. St Pancras (1876) with its superb detail, castellated fringes, clock tower and numerous pointed-arch windows and chimneys is a superb English example.

Train near Nottingham Midland Station, 1839. (Picture the Past, NTGM009692)

The final stage, 1890 to 1914, is 'Megalomania' where towns and cities tried to outdo each other by building even bigger and more flamboyant stations. Impressive hotels were sometimes incorporated into the structures, with entrances often graced by enormous arches. Paris's Gare d'Orsay (1900) and Copenhagen Central (1911) are good examples, while Valencia's Estacion del Norte's (1906–17) intricate detail is illustrative of the growing influence of Art Nouveau, fine, intricate metalwork, rounded domes, soft curves and dainty ornamentation (see p. 56).

Nottingham's splendid Midland Station, with elements of art nouveau in its ironwork gates and railings, is an excellent monument to the huge influence of railways in the county.

After the First World War the motor car came to be seen as the future and eventually concrete lines greatly outnumbered steel ones. New stations reflected this new age of functionality by being constructed with concrete, plastic and steel in unimaginative styles.

Visiting

The station is open every day for passengers. There is no guide leaflet as yet but there is an excellent café in the main hall. Also stroll down Station Road, cross London Road and look at the recently restored terminus of the Great Northern branch-line from Grantham. Designed by T.C. Hine, it opened in 1857 to serve the Ambergate, Nottingham, Boston and Eastern Junction Railway. It became a goods depot and is now a nightclub. A Civic Society pamphlet by J.P. Wilson has a good map of Nottingham's railway system around 1910 with great pictures.

Valencia Station.

NEWARK CASTLE

In his list of fifty-eight castles to visit, Trevor Yorke, in *English Castles Explained*, doesn't mention one in Nottinghamshire. This county's castles are not impressive – now. Nottingham's and Newark's would have been 500 years ago, but by then the usefulness of castles was in decline. Once the means by which the local lord could establish his authority over an area, and in which he, his family and his paid army of retainers lived, the castle was becoming outdated by the sixteenth century. Susceptible to cannon fire, they were also draughty and expensive to run.

Both Nottingham and Newark Castles, although decayed, were still grand enough to play a key role in the Civil War (1642-49). Across the country, castles, whether derelict or still occupied, were refortified and used as bases for the opposing forces. After their victory over the Royalists, the Parliamentary forces partially or totally demolished castles to prevent their potential use in any future conflicts (even Windsor Castle faced a Parliamentary Bill for its destruction – defeated by one vote). Those castles spared were mainly held by Parliamentary troops and essential to the defences of the country. Hence Windsor and Dover Castles are still in such good condition today. Nottingham's castle was demolished to make way for a stately mansion, but Newark's remains were left in sufficient grandeur to dominate over the River Trent even today. The original Norman castle was erected in the 1070s and rebuilt in stone after 1123 by Bishop Alexander the Magnificent. Its northern gateway is the best-preserved Norman castle gatehouse in Britain.

Civil War

In the English Civil War of 1642-49 the castle was an important Royalist garrison, holding out against sieges in 1643 and 1644. In 1645, following their victory at Naseby in June, the

Parliamentarians pushed towards Newark again. They passed Shelford House (Notts), garrisoned by around 200 Royalist troops, led by Colonel Stanhope. Told to surrender, he replied, 'I keep this garrison for the King and in defence of it I will live and die'. He was cut down along with 140 of his men. The Parliamentary army went on to capture Belvoir Castle and, in November, surrounded Newark. By May 1646, the situation was hopeless for King Charles and he went, disguised as a woman, to meet with the Scottish Army, hoping to deal with them. He met them at the Saracens Head, Southwell, a lovely former coaching inn, still there today. The Scots handed Charles over to the Parliamentarians, and Charles ordered Newark to surrender. The first part of the Civil War was over and the castle dismantling commenced, but, luckily, was interrupted by an outbreak of plague.

Other Civil Wars in English History

- 1135–54 – King Stephen vs Queen Matilda. Before his death in 1135, Henry I named his daughter, Matilda, as heir to the throne and forced his barons to swear allegiance to her. Many barons preferred Stephen, the King's nephew, and England descended into a period of anarchy and civil war during which over 1,100 fortifications were built. Most were demolished after hostilities ended in 1153 when Stephen recognised Matilda's son, Henry, as his heir. Stephen died in 1154 and Henry III's reign commenced.

Newark Castle.

- 1215-17 – Barons' rebellion. Reacting to King John's constant demands for money to fight his French wars, the barons forced the King to sign the Magna Carta. However, after a few months, civil war broke out between the rebel barons and the King. The rebels invited Louis, heir to the French throne, to help them. In May 1216, Louis invaded the country, marched into London and was proclaimed King, although not crowned. By 14 June he had captured Winchester and had control over half of the British kingdom. In October, John died at Newark Castle and many barons, worried by the influence of the French Army, switched their allegiance to John's nine-year-old son. The two sides fought each other for a year before the young boy was crowned Henry III and the French went back home.

- 1264-67 – Second Barons' rebellion. Once again provoked by the King's demand for money, many barons, led by Simon De Montfort, forced the King to sign the Provisions of Oxford, which gave them some key powers and compelled the King to call Parliament every three years. Once again the two sides came to battle. Henry III was defeated at the Battle of Lewes in 1264 and De Montfort ruled England for a time. However in 1265 the Royalists regrouped and, at the Battle of Evesham, De Montfort was killed. Thereafter, savage retribution was exacted on the rebels and Henry was restored as King.

- 1455-87 – Wars of the Roses. See Battle of Stoke Field.

Visiting

There is an excellent visitor centre with visual displays. Also there are Victorian Gardens for special events and historical re-enactments. Both open daily. Dungeons and towers tours are available (best book in advance). Contact for charges and details (01636 655765).

NEWARK OLD TOWN

In 1964 the Council for British Archaeology included Newark in its list of fifty-one British towns of outstanding historic quality. It is not hard to see why. The castle and St Mary's Church are already listed as individual sites, but there is more. Newark's visitor centre is the place to start, being complete with displays, free leaflets and all the information you need to get acquainted with the choices – a Civil War Trail, a Town Trail, industrial heritage sites, and two good museums.

This entry concentrates on the Old Town, i.e. that part of the centre that used to be enclosed by the medieval defences, which were probably initially just an earth bank and a ditch. A stone wall was probably added in the fourteenth century, the entry gates being at Bridge Street, Bargate and Mill Gate. Use the map in the free 'Civil War Trail' leaflet to trace the old wall's borders – along Castle Gate, Slaughter House Lane/The Mount, Carter Gate and Lombard Street. Unfortunately, like the Roman road, nothing remains to be seen today except the layout.

The Old Town is a compact area encompassing many historical buildings, but few are medieval now. Like most towns, it contains a mixture of styles – Georgian, Victorian and modern, all on view around the lovely Market Square. Newark, however, does have more timber-framed buildings than most places and certainly more than the other Nottinghamshire towns. Not all the timber-framed buildings are pre-sixteenth century but several are. An inexpensive leaflet issued

The White Hart, Newark.

by the Newark Civic Trust entitled 'Look at Newark On Trent' is a good basic guide to many of the old buildings and explains the origin of the town from a Roman settlement of some kind (apart from the four on the Fosse Way) to an important Anglo-Saxon site (judging from the large fifth- or sixth-century cemetery excavated in Mill Gate). It also states that 'the modern town was planned by Bishop Alexander (1123-48), who built the castle and bridged the Trent… and… laid out the Market Place'. The highly-regarded historian Pevsner thought Newark's street plan a good example of a town planned by a Norman bishop.

Timber-Framed Buildings
Newark has some very good examples accessible to the public:

- Woolpack Inn, Stodman Street – fifteenth-century building containing a full set of original medieval rafters. Beneath the front render probably lies a 'close-studded' timber frame.

- 22-24 Kirkgate – much restored, but material in the upper floor dates to 1337.

- Old White Hart – medieval timber-framed building of national importance, it has the oldest example of a crown post roof (the most popular form of roof in the medieval period) in the county, and has been dated to 1313. Possibly constructed to be a merchant's house, it became an inn in the late fourteenth century. The oldest part now houses an estate agent.

- The Governor's House, Lombard Street – a splendid fifteenth-century, three-storey building, with each storey jettied out beyond the one below. Now a tearoom, so you can see the interior too.

Why are they important? In the Middle Ages, the only buildings made from stone would have been castles, churches, monasteries and some manor houses. Houses for ordinary folk, even important ones, were generally made of timber, with wattle and daub infilling for the walls.

Timber was originally used because it was plentiful. By the fifteenth century, after years of use for smelting and shipbuilding, it was becoming scarcer. The price of timber rose and a new material began to be imported from Holland – brick. At first, brick was used in the construction of large country houses such as Holme Pierrepont (around 1500). In the early seventeenth century, Thrumpton Hall (1608) and Clifton Hall (1630) were built entirely of brick. After bricks began to be made locally, they became cheaper and were used for more ordinary dwellings. In the eighteenth and nineteenth centuries, while the Georgian kings and Queen Victoria ruled the country, industry thrived, population soared and, all over the country, houses and factories sprung up to change the face of the land. Most of them were made of brick or locally-sourced stone. Even if the older timber houses had remained they would have been vastly outnumbered. Unfortunately, most were knocked down to make way for new buildings or rebuilt with new materials. We now have to rely on the few remaining ones to provide us with an insight into everyday living in the eleventh to seventeenth centuries. Good places to see timber buildings today include York, Chester and Shrewsbury.

Coaching Inns

By 1800 the town had five cotton mills, 700 stocking frames, an iron foundry, a wool trade, a linen-weaving industry and much malt trade, as well as over twenty windmills in the vicinity. The River Trent helped it grow, bringing in timber, grain and coal and taking out malt, flour and plaster. Improvements to the roads by the turnpikes enabled Newark to become a route centre, with seven coaches per day running along the Great North Road to and from London, as well as traffic between Lincoln and Nottingham and all the local private coaches and farmers' carts.

Many travellers needed somewhere to stay. Newark had three coaching inns around its busy square – the Old White Hart, the Saracen's Head and the Clinton Arms (as well as others around the town). More information on them is in the guides, but if you could time your visit to the early nineteenth century you could spend a fascinating few hours watching the hustle and bustle as the horse-teams haul the coaches into the square and manoeuvre them through narrow gateways into the coach yards at the rear of the inns. Some older local people would have done just that. They would listen for the post horn announcing the arrival of the mail coach and watch the ostlers rush to prepare a fresh batch of horses. The coachman, wrapped in a large overcoat, would put away his whip and scramble down from the box to join his passengers as they hurried into the inn needing to relieve themselves and grab something to eat quickly. The coach could be ready to move on, with a fresh team of horses, within ten minutes.

Mail coaches would have been a frequent sight in the square. To increase speeds, mail coaches did not have to stop and pay tolls on turnpike roads, they just sounded their horn and the gates were opened. At one time twenty-five were leaving London every night to carry mail across the country. They must have looked a splendid sight in black and maroon livery with a Royal Mail badge on the side, along with route details, such as 'London-York'.

Visiting

Nottinghamshire Heritage Gateway's internet site has an excellent summary of Newark by Andy Nicholson, including references for further reading. See also *Timber Framed Buildings of Nottinghamshire* by Jason Mordan. Every day at Newark is Market Day except Tuesday.

ST MARY'S CHURCH, NEWARK

This church could easily be mistaken for a cathedral – it looks the part, inside and out. However, along with St Mary's of Nottingham, it is in the diocese of Southwell, with its inspiring cathedral, so a church it will remain. According to the famous architectural historian, Nikolaus Pevsner, it is, 'Among the two or three dozen grandest parish churches of England'. It began as a modestly-sized, aisle-less building, erected on the site of a former Saxon church, but from 1230 it was rebuilt. Newark was an important wool town in the Middle Ages and the wealthy wool and cloth merchants would have helped fund the project. One rich merchant, Alan Fleming, died in 1363 and a brass to his memory lies in the church, one of only a dozen Flemish-made brasses in the country. The rebuilding took 200 years and as a result the church incorporates a number of styles. It also has a lovely 252ft spire, and two chantry chapels dating to the early sixteenth century, which provide us with an insight into how people thought in the thirteenth and fourteenth centuries.

The Fleming Brass.

Chantries and Purgatory

A chantry is an altar or chapel set up, generally within a church, by a private individual, who would provide the funds for a priest to pray for their soul whilst it was in purgatory. The concept of purgatory is a belief unique to the Roman Catholic Church. Catholics believe that salvation is a gradual process and that few people go direct to Heaven. First they have to spend a period of time in purgatory, being cleansed of their sins. If their sins have harmed others then the period of time will be longer. However, if friends, family or others pray for them, it might help speed things up. Many Protestant Christians believe, on the other hand, that salvation and transfer to Heaven at death is achieved by repenting of their sins and trusting in Jesus Christ during their lifetime.

As well as regular prayers for their soul, the chantry builders hoped their buildings would indicate the sincerity of their repentance and help them gain forgiveness. For example, William the Conqueror built a monastery at the site of his famous victory over King Harold (Battle Abbey), and also encouraged the building of new churches throughout the country, almost certainly hoping to atone for his intrigues and aggression.

In the fourteenth and fifteenth centuries it was felt that many monks and monasteries were slipping from their high ideals, so rich landowners and merchants began to put their money into their local church instead. In A.C. Wood's words, 'Chancels were enlarged or rebuilt, side aisles were added, great windows of many lights replaced the narrow slits of earlier times, elaborately carved easter sepulches, sedelia and rood screens were introduced'. And inside these larger and more intricately decorated churches, the wealthy would install their chantries, with priests to chant daily masses for the souls of the founder and their families. Those slightly less well-off would provide for a priest to say a yearly mass (an obit) at their altar, or for a light to be kept burning. By the end of the fifteenth century, Wood estimates between seventy and eighty priests were paid to say prayers at altars in thirty local churches (thirteen at Southwell). St Mary's, Nottingham, had three chantries, St Nicholas's in Tuxford had two, but St Mary's of Newark had fifteen chantries. The practice was widespread in the country – by 1547, York Minster had around fifty chantries.

Another way of reducing one's time in purgatory was to view ancient religious artefacts. In 1520 the Castle Church, Wittenburg, Germany, held one of Europe's largest collections of these relics (19,000 items) including vials of the milk of the Virgin Mary, straw from the manger and the body of one of the innocents massacred by King Herod. By donating toward the preservation of the Castle Church, a person could receive an indulgence of 100 days per relic visited. If they managed to visit every relic, they could reduce their time in purgatory by 5,209 years!

Indulgences

Around the thirteenth century the Church came up with a new way for some people to obtain forgiveness – indulgences. The theory was that good works performed by the clergy and monks left the Church in credit as regards to forgiveness. They could therefore sell off some of this surplus to those they felt needed it – a tempting idea for both parties. The Church gained much needed cash and the buyer of the indulgence received a piece of paper signed by a bishop stating that the Church had performed good works on his or her behalf. Effectively, the person was buying the right to spend less time in purgatory.

From the start there were critics because the rich could buy off their sins, while the poor had to rely solely on their own efforts. John Wycliffe (1320-84) argued that God alone could forgive sins. His supporters (Lollards) travelled throughout the land preaching his message. This was seen as heretical at the time and, forty-four years after his death, the Pope ordered Wycliffe's bones to be dug up and burnt. However, Wycliffe's writings inspired later thinkers such as Martin Luther (1483-1546). Luther's role in the Reformation has been well-documented, but essentially he rejected the idea of purgatory and the system of indulgences, along with other criticisms of Church practice. On the continent this led to the spread of the Protestant Church, which itself eventually split into many different factions.

Two Survive

In the 1530s Henry VIII took the English Church out of the Pope's control, closed down all the monasteries and confiscated their land and possessions. He toyed with Protestant ideas, including the rejection of purgatory, and took the opportunity in 1545 to appropriate the chantries and the money set aside to pay for them. His successor, Edward VI, completed the job and 2,000 chantries were dissolved. In Nottinghamshire over fifty chantries, chapels, etc. disappeared and fifty-eight priests who had served them lost their jobs. However, some of the money helped establish grammar schools in Mansfield and East Retford, and some went towards the maintenance of Trent Bridge.

Two of St Mary's chantries can still be seen today either side of the High Altar, both built over the tombs of their benefactors. On the south side is the chapel provided by the will of Robert Markham in 1505, while on the north is the chapel provided by the will of Thomas Mering of Newark in 1500. Thomas left 'all my clipped wole and all my floke of shepe' to pay for it.

Visiting

Visitors who appreciate that this is a working church are welcome. Monday-Saturday, 9 a.m.-4 p.m. (closed for lunch) and Sunday afternoons. A good guidebook is available.

NEWSTEAD ABBEY

Newstead Abbey is best known for a person who lived there for a few years in the early nineteenth century, George Byron. However, it began life in the twelfth century as an Augustinian priory, 800 years after the first Christian monasteries began to appear in Egypt. The west front still stands, the best surviving relic of the great age of Norman monastery-building in the county. By the end of the twelfth century, there were twelve such monasteries thriving in Nottinghamshire and hundreds throughout the land. These splendid landmarks fell victim to Henry VIII's desire to wed Anne Boleyn. His desire produced Queen Elizabeth, the Protestant Church and a land full of monastic ruins.

Before 1536 there were about 850 monastic houses in England. Most were built in the twelfth and thirteenth centuries, the period that saw the erection of thousands of stone castles, churches and monasteries throughout Europe. From 1536 to 1541, most of the English monasteries were destroyed. Spectacular remains can be seen at Fountains Abbey and Rievaulx Abbey, both in North Yorkshire, but there are also many less spectacular ruins spread over the country. They serve as a reminder of the essence of the Middle Ages, a time when to be learned or to able to read and write meant you were almost certainly a member of the clergy or a monk; a time before the discovery of the New World, when knowledge of lands beyond the Near East was hazy; a time when the local church dominated peoples' lives. Careful – a trip to Newstead's splendid arch could lead you into this time!

Henry VIII confiscated Newstead's abbey and lands and sold them to Sir John Byron in 1540. They remained in the Byron family for 300 years. John converted the building for his own use, but kept much of the original structure and monastic layout so that the house today still retains a medieval character. Subsequent alterations and renovations have left the building now attached to the abbey-front very much Byron's residence.

Byrons and Luddites

The 5th Lord Byron was known as 'the Wicked Lord'. He spent his fortune on travel, art and improving the building and estate. He increased the size of the lake and used it to stage mock naval battles. In the space of a few years he was found guilty of manslaughter after a coffee house dispute, and learnt that his son had married an impecunious lady. He retired to a small apartment in the south-east wing, sold off much of the house's contents and let the building decay. In 1798 he died, predeceased by his son, and the property passed to the 6th Lord, George Byron, who took residence when he turned twenty-one in 1808.

In 1812, George Byron returned from a two-year tour of Europe and made his maiden speech in the House of Lords on behalf of the Luddites. Thousands of people in Nottinghamshire earned a meagre living by producing stockings on a stocking frame. Much of the work was done in homes with upper-floor windows made bigger for extra light. When manufacturers brought in cut-ups – the stocking not knitted to shape, but knitted straight, cut out, and then seamed together – output increased and prices dropped. The majority of stockingers who produced

Newstead Abbey.

the genuine article were devastated. After four years of bad harvests and increased food prices it was too much; many were at starvation level and had to apply for Poor Relief. Ned Ludlam, a Leicester apprentice, smashed his stocking frame in a temper and the Luddite movement began. At Arnold, Nottingham, on 11 March 1811, a group of Luddites broke sixty-three frames and this was followed by further acts of violence against the frames of those suspected of producing 'cut-ups'. A Bill was brought in to impose the death penalty for frame-breaking and Byron spoke out against it in the House of Lords: 'I have been in some of the most oppressed provinces in Turkey; but never under the most despotic of infidel governments did I behold such squalid wretchedness as I have seen since my return to the very heart of a Christian country.' Shortly after this his 'Childe Harold's Progress' was published. People liked his exciting style of poetry and he became a celebrity almost overnight.

Byron was famous as much for his lifestyle as for his writing. He had a number of scandalous affairs, ran up huge debts (in 1817 he sold Newstead to free himself from debt), and loved to engage in acts of physical bravado. He swam the Thames from Lambeth to Blackfriars for a bet, the Grand Canal in Venice to win a race, and across the Hellespont to emulate Leander. Near the end of his life he moved to Greece, possibly to escape another affair, and aligned himself with the Greeks fighting a war of independence against the Ottoman Empire. He died from a fever in 1824 after being bled by leeches (the standard treatment of the time) and is regarded by many there as a national hero. His best known work is 'Don Juan', and fans come from all over the world to visit Newstead, Southwell (where he spent his school vacations) and his final resting place, Hucknall Church.

Others

Thomas Wildman, an old school friend of George, bought the property in 1817 and used his fortune from plantations in Jamaica to restore it. The next owner, William Webb, installed gas lighting, central heating and trophies from his African hunting expeditions, which gave the house an exotic look. One of the visitors at this time was Dr Livingstone, who had saved Webb's life when the pair of them were in Africa. Webb's grandson, Charles Ian Fraser, sold it to the Nottinghamshire philanthropist Sir Julien Cahn, who presented it to Nottingham Corporation in 1931.

Visiting

Newstead has medieval cloisters, splendid Victorian room settings, an excellent café and ten different styles of garden, set around lakes and parkland. House open 1 April–30 September, 12 p.m. to 5 p.m. Grounds open 9 a.m. to 6 p.m. daily, except the last Friday in November and Christmas Day. Telephone for admission charges (01623 455900).

NOTINTONE PLACE

Not awe-inspiring at first glance, Notintone Place is odd and not just because of the name. In an area much redeveloped, this small remaining section of a long row of houses looks as if it has been preserved for a reason. It has. It is the birthplace (1829) of one of the most remarkable individuals of the nineteenth century. We are introduced to his story through the museum now inhabiting the building, which leaves you appreciative of William Booth's splendid statue in the front courtyard. The pages of the visitors' book are dominated by tributes from South Africa, Australia, Canada, the Philippines, Sweden, etc., demonstrating the impact he made around the world. William Booth is one of the great figures in history, whose influence for good is still being felt today. His story is yet another illustration of the heroic helpers of the nineteenth century.

As a boy, Booth attended Mr Biddulph's school in a building now occupied by the Lace Market Theatre. At age thirteen, a year before his father died, he was apprenticed to a pawnbroker in Goosegate, where he learned of the terrible difficulties faced by the poor. Despite disliking his job, he worked for seven years to support his mother, who ran a corner shop to make ends meet. At age fifteen, William became a Methodist after visits to the Wesleyan chapel on Broad Street (now the Broadway Media Centre). Capable of holding 2,500 people, it was often packed by those listening to the many, powerful, travelling speakers (the pop stars of today). William Booth said of one of them, James Caughey, 'He was an extraordinary preacher... there were such crowds and rushes to hear the Gospel as we had never dreamed of seeing. There were wonderful meetings, wonderful influences, and wonderful conversions'. (G. Railton, *Twenty-One Years' Salvation Army, 1891*, p. 8) A plaque commemorating Booth's conversion is preserved on the wall inside the cinema today.

Booth still at Notintone Place.

The Rise of Nonconformists

The eighteenth and nineteenth centuries saw a great rise in the number of Nonconformist churches following the Act of Toleration of 1689. As the population increased and workers increasingly moved into overcrowded towns, these urban working classes were cut off from their old village church. Some lost the habit of regular attendance. Others sought new churches because the established church clergy lacked enthusiasm and passion and the middle-class congregations did not always welcome workers from the tightly-packed, unhealthy and disease-ridden areas of town. Other religious outlets grew to fill the gap, one being the Methodists. John Wesley (1703-91) preached the gospel and personal salvation by faith to those without religion. Shunned by many in the established church, he preached in the open air and his passion converted thousands of urban poor to his cause. By 1815 there were nearly 250,000 Wesleyan Methodists in Great Britain and over 200,000 in the United States, most with a chapel in their own town.

Booth Inspired

Booth worked as a travelling Methodist preacher after his marriage in 1855. Ten years later, after increasingly being drawn to those at the bottom of the pile, those in the worst slums, he began his own Christian mission. At first it was one of a great many groups trying to help feed and clothe the poor in the East End. But Booth was inspirational. A great speaker, he drew others to join him. His army grew. As well as providing shelter and food for the poor, he set up a labour exchange and a missing persons' bureau. His army tackled problems that others shied away from. They campaigned against drink and young girls being sold into prostitution. For this they suffered the wrath of the publicans and brothel keepers, who organised intimidation such as the throwing of eggs and stones at the volunteers.

An Army is Born

In 1878 William summoned his son, Branwell, and friend, George Railton, to read the proof of his mission's annual report. The report included a statement: 'The Christian Mission is a Volunteer Army', to which they objected. The word 'volunteer' was very much associated with part-time soldiers in Queen Victoria's army. Branwell and Railton insisted they were regulars, not part-timers, compelled to do their job through passion. William replaced the word 'volunteer' with 'salvation'. His helpers liked being associated with an army fighting crime and poverty; the name stuck and the Salvation Army grew and grew.

Far and Wide

Towards the end of the nineteenth century, shelters opened in Brussels and Copenhagen. In 1895, Booth held 340 meetings in eighty-six cities across America, where the Army filled the need for religion in the fast expanding cities. He even addressed the US Senate. It spread to help the poor and disadvantaged throughout Europe (the Kings of Norway and Sweden went to meet him) and to Australia and Japan. When he died, 40,000 attended his funeral and wreaths were laid by the King, the US Ambassador and Kaiser Wilhelm.

Today it has operations in over 110 countries, as well as over 800 caring centres in the UK and Ireland with more than 4,000 employees and an army of volunteers. This is an exciting and inspiring story, well worth looking up in one of the books of his life.

To Help or Not to Help?

The Industrial Revolution caused much suffering for millions of people; long working hours, harsh working conditions, squalid housing in overcrowded slums with little or no sewage disposal systems and contaminated water supplies. Who was to blame? Many of those in power thought that individuals were responsible for their own lives. If people were industrious, thrifty and refrained from vices such as drinking and gambling, then they would prosper. Others saw that thousands of people could be swamped by circumstances beyond their control. In an age before the welfare state, some individuals came to feel they had a duty to help those less fortunate than themselves.

William Booth was one of a number of heroic helpers, each inspired by religious belief, who came to be known as Evangelicals. Lord Shaftsbury (1801-85) devoted his life to reform and was the power behind many of the Factory Acts, including the 1842 Mines Act banning the employment of children underground. Thomas Barnardo (1845-1905) set up homes to rescue hundreds of poor, homeless children. William Wilberforce (1755-1833) worked long and hard to abolish the slave trade. Elizabeth Fry (1780-1845) worked tirelessly for prison reform.

Saved

In 1938, Notintone Place provided emergency accommodation for stranded girls or women, although the bedroom of Booth's birth was kept as a memorial. In the 1960s the area was destined for demolition, but the Salvation Army protested. This small group of houses was spared – another battle won. They added an elderly persons' home/goodwill centre, and a museum in 1971.

Visiting

This is a working complex with friendly staff, but no facilities other than postcards. Phone to ensure the museum will be open (0115 9503927). Be sure to make a voluntary contribution.

ST MARY'S CHURCH, NOTTINGHAM

St Mary's, the senior church in the city, is the venue for important civic services, including the welcome to the new Lord Mayor of Nottingham each year. One of the best 'non-cathedrals' in the land, its history can be traced back to before the Norman Conquest through the Domesday Book records. This lends weight to the theory that it was once the site of an old English minster church, possibly ninth century or earlier. A splendid site, its history is linked to Nottingham's development. Try also to see the two other city centre churches, St Peter's and St Nicholas's, as they are all part of the same story.

Two Towns

Nottingham's site, on top of the highest point of the sandstone spur overlooking a fording place on the River Trent, attracted the Danish Vikings in the 860s. It had defensive features on three sides: a steep cliff to the south, the River Beck to the east and an escarpment to the west. By AD 877, the Danes controlled the emerging shires of Lincoln, Leicester, Derby and Nottingham which, together with Stamford, made up the Five Boroughs. A.C. Wood, in his excellent *A History of Nottinghamshire*, asserts that, the Danes being heathens, 'it is certain that their invasion brought destruction to most of the churches and religious houses in the Danelaw'.

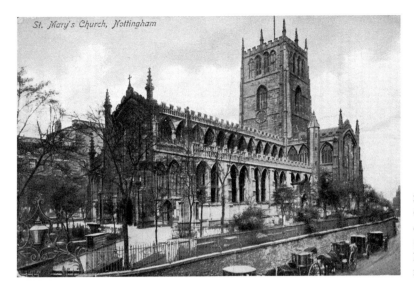

St Mary's
Church,
early 1900s.
(Courtesy of
Picture the Past,
NTGM010366)

But, 'in the tenth century the mass of the new settlers were won over to Christianity and... the structure of the Church in the Danelaw was once more erected'.

A bridge was constructed over the Trent in AD 920 – the settlement was growing. Almost certainly the inhabitants of the fortified burh prayed in a church that stood on the current site of St Mary's. After the Norman takeover of 1066, William Peverel was granted the 'Honour of Nottingham', which meant he ruled his area, subject to the King. Peverel built the castle, around which houses grew up for the members of the garrison, their families and the traders who supplied them. This French area also had its own churches, St Peter's and St Nicholas's . So two separate towns developed – the 'French Borough' and 'the English Borough', each with its own sheriff, a practice that continued until 1835! A market place developed (today's Market Square) where they met, and eventually the enlarged town was protected by a Norman ditch and earthworks.

Three Churches

In Norman times all three churches were under the control of Lenton Priory and remained so until the county's most important monastery was destroyed in 1538. Before then the churches were burnt down during the Civil War of 1135-53 when Matilda fought Stephen for the throne. In 1140 Matilda's forces failed to capture Nottingham Castle, set fire to the town and all three churches were destroyed. They were destroyed again in 1153, just before Matilda's son, Henry II, became King. Henry II was a much stronger King than Stephen but even he faced a rebellion. Some of his barons seized Nottingham Castle in 1173 and sacked the town. Henry soon regained control, but meanwhile the churches had been damaged yet again.

All three churches were rebuilt soon after 1175. The St Mary's we see today however, is not the one that was rebuilt at that time. It was completely rebuilt again at the end of the reign of Edward III (1327-77). The late fourteenth century was a time of prosperity for the English spinning and weaving towns so it would have been relatively easy to raise money for the work. The project finally came to an end with the completion of the tower, around the same time as Christopher Columbus was rediscovering America in 1492. So as not to disrupt the daily life of the parishioners, the new church was built around the old one, which was then demolished. Very little of the old building remains, but there is a stone frame of a two-light church window, built into a factory wall (on Broadway) in the Lace Market, that is from the old church.

In the nineteenth century, the Danish part of town developed into the world's most famous lace manufacturing area, and St Mary's Church was in the centre of the action. In the twentieth century, the lace industry declined and St Mary's was left in the shade. The redevelopment of the former Lace Market is now bringing the area back into the mainstream. For the shoppers who flock to the town from the suburbs however, the position of St Mary's is such that very few get to see it, or even know that it is there.

St Peter's Church is in the most commanding position of the modern-day city, being right next to Marks & Spencers, yet most people do not notice it because they are too busy shopping. This impressive chuch claims to be the oldest building in continuous use in Nottingham. Since it was rebuilt in the fourteenth century, it has remained substantially the same despite restoration work in 1886 to improve safety. The oldest part of the church, the south arcade, dates to around 1180, and the north arcade is fourteenth century.

Of the rebuilt fourteenth-century St Nicholas's Church, we know little, because it was demolished during the seventeenth century Civil War. It had been used by snipers to fire on the castle and had to go! The rebuilding in brick began after the end of the war in 1671 and was completed in 1682.

Visiting

For St Peter's and St Mary's, where you can try your hand at brass rubbing, check opening details in advance (0115 9483658). For St Nicholas's, contact for further information (0115 9524600).

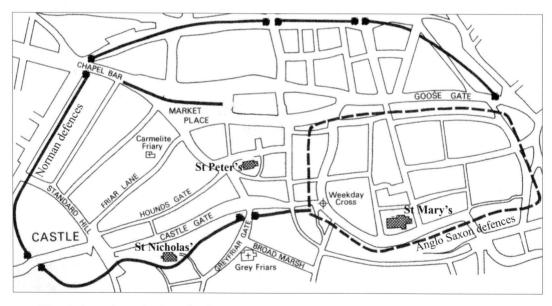

Historical map shows the three churches serving the Norman castle, the city centre and the Anglo-Saxon town. The defensive walls and friaries no longer exist and the street pattern is early twentieth century, before Maid Marion Way cut through from Chapel Bar, past St Nicholas' Church to the new Broad Marsh Centre.

NOTTINGHAM CASTLE

William the Conqueror took control of the country in 1066 and although the cream of the Anglo-Saxon warriors had been decimated at Fulford, Stamford Bridge and Hastings, he started a massive castle-building programme as a warning that any attempts to rise up against him would be met with force. Nottingham, London, Warwick, Lincoln and York were amongst the first castles built, and by the time of William's death in 1087, there were eighty-six Norman castles in England.

Nottingham's first castle was a motte-and-bailey type surrounded by a wooden palisade. In the twelfth century it was rebuilt in stone by Henry I, and, complete with towers, moat and drawbridge, it became one of the main fortresses of the Midlands and a favoured residence for England's kings and queens during the medieval period. While Richard the Lionheart was in captivity abroad in 1194, his brother John ruled much of the land from this castle (making frequent hunting trips to Sherwood Forest, staying at Clipstone Palace). When Richard finally returned, John was none too pleased and refused to surrender his castles. Richard forced their surrender until only Nottingham held out. Then he led an assault which captured some defenders. The next day he hung several of these prisoners in full view of the castle. The message was clear. The castle soon surrendered and John was banished from England.

On Richard's death, John became King and in 1212 the castle witnessed arguably its darkest day. John was holding twenty-eight boys hostage as a guarantee of Welsh Prince Llewellyn's good behaviour. On hearing of a revolt by Llewellyn, he became very angry and ordered all the boys to be hung from the castle walls.

Impressive Site

As Nottingham folk know, it is no longer a castle. Along with many other castles, refortified for the Civil War, it had its main structures destroyed by order of Parliament (see Newark Castle). Unlike Newark, its remains were cleared to make way for a new mansion, so little of the stone castle remains. Why then is this site so important? It is now an impressive ducal mansion, restored and adapted into a museum by Nottingham's famous architect, T.C. Hine, after being gutted by fire during the Reform Act Riots of 1831 (see Nottingham Market Square). It was the first municipal art gallery in the country outside London (opened in 1878), and also has a good museum showing the story of Nottingham. But it is the site itself and its history that impresses. Built on a high, natural sandstone ridge, overlooking a strategic crossing point on the River Trent, it is the best natural defensive site in the county and one of the best in the country. The site was ripe for a castle. The caves and secret passages are still there, as are the views from the top, the castle grounds, the restored medieval gatehouse and, of course, the legend of Robin Hood (personified by Robin's statue below the castle rock). If we are to believe the legends, Robin fought against the sheriff here in the twelfth or thirteenth century – see the display in the museum.

Threats and Wars

Let us add some more events that actually occurred here. In August 1485, a messenger rushed into the castle with urgent news for King Richard III. Henry Tudor had landed in Wales and was marching to Lichfield, amassing recruits along the way. Here was a real threat to the King , as sentiment in the country had turned against him after rumours circulated that he had murdered two young princes in the Tower. From the castle he sent out messages to all his supporters to come

The castle, *c.* 1500. (Courtesy of Picture the Past, NTGM002829)

join him, and the very next day he and his army set out with banners flying and drums beating to Leicester. From there, Richard advanced to Bosworth Field and his death. The victor, Henry Tudor, Earl of Richmond, was crowned on the battlefield as Henry VII. Henry, sensing that strong castles across the land, such as Nottingham, were a menace to his rule, allowed them to fall into disuse.

At the outbreak of the Civil War (1642-46) many castles in various stages of disrepair were patched up and used again. Nottingham, where Charles I raised his flag and attempted to recruit an army, was one of them. Few came forward and Nottingham eventually declared for Parliament. Newark sided with the Royalists, along with most of the county's large country houses, so Colonel Hutchinson had a very difficult job to hold the castle and keep Trent Bridge open for his side. He did so heroically, finishing on the winning side, whereas Newark eventually surrendered.

Mortimer's Hole

Be sure not to miss the tour of the caves, which includes the secret passage through which the conspirators crept in 1330 to capture Roger Mortimer. Edward II (1307-27) quarrelled with Mortimer, one of his powerful barons, and imprisoned him in 1322. But he escaped captivity in 1324 and fled to France. There he met King Edward's wife, Isabella, and they commenced a passionate affair which became the scandal of Western Europe. Knowing Edward was very unpopular in England, Mortimer and Isabella decided to return in 1326 to confront him. Edward was forced to abdicate, imprisoned in Berkeley Castle and brutally murdered. For the next three years, Mortimer and Isabella ruled the country in the name of Prince Edward, still in his teens. In 1330 the supporters of the Prince fought back. They gained entry to the castle via a little-known passage, struck down two guards and dragged Mortimer and his lover away to London. On the 29 November 1330 he was hung, drawn and quartered at Tyburn.

There are great views, good displays about the castle and its history, and good facilities. Check times of cave-tours (0115 9153700). Open daily. Entrance fee includes access to Brewhouse Yard Museum and caves.

As well as Nottingham, Newark and Laxton, the county had castles at Worksop, Bothamsall, Egmanton, Annesley, Lowdham, Aslockton, Cuckney and Kirkby in Ashfield. For details try *The Castles of Nottinghamshire* by James Wright, or *Nottingham's Royal Castle* by Andrew Hamilton.

NOTTINGHAM MARKET SQUARE

Nottingham's Old Market Square is impressive. Its 2007 makeover has opened it out and made it look large enough to have been the venue for the annual Goose Fair, which it was until 1927. But how large is it? According to one website it is one of the top forty largest squares in the European Union and one of the top seventy in the world. At 22,000 sq. metres it is also reputed to be the largest square in England, Trafalgar coming in second at a measly 12,100 sq. metres. This is an area, however, open to debate. Firstly, should a square be defined as a predominantly paved, open space? If so, then Lincoln's Inn Fields, London, approximately 28,000 sq. metres in size, but with much of it grassed (as are many of London's squares), can be ignored.

Secondly, while many squares have structures within them, most do not include a large building. Nottingham's figure includes the area upon which the Council House stands. Opened in 1929 by the Prince of Wales, it replaced the New Exchange Buildings erected on the site in the 1720s. Even in the earliest map of the town (John Speed's of 1610), there were houses situated there. If we remove that area from the calculations, but leave in much of Long Row, arguably very much part of the square, we are left with around 13,000 sq. metres. That would still leave it in first place in England.

Squares

The word 'square' derives from the French *esquare* (Latin *exquadro*), to give a square shape. Although squares have been a feature of European towns and cities for over 2,000 years, the word has become associated with the feature, not the shape. Squares come in a variety of shapes, including circular, but most are not square. They began as market places in larger towns, generally sited in the centre where major routes would tend to meet. These areas would attract large structures such as Town Halls and statues. Mansfield, Newark and Retford all have attractive town squares with civic buildings.

Origins

The Norman conquerors chose Nottingham's square to suit their followers who manned the castle and lived in the small settlement that grew up around it. When these folk went to the market at Weekday Cross in the Anglian town, there was friction between them and the locals. To prevent trouble, a new place was found within reach of the castle guards and a new market square was laid out, which wasn't square. A wall was constructed across the market to separate the English, who took the Long Row side, and the French, and certain passages were made through it to facilitate trade. The remains of this dividing wall were not swept away until 1713.

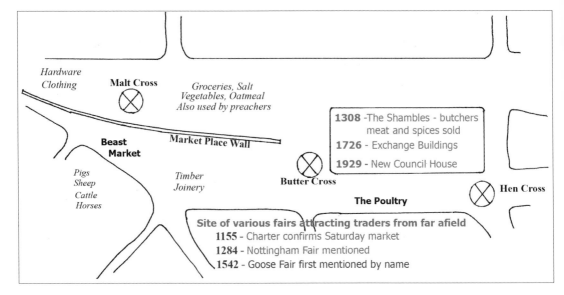

Map of medieval square showing market crosses, dividing wall, etc.

The map contains the following labels:

Hardware Clothing

Malt Cross

Groceries, Salt Vegetables, Oatmeal Also used by preachers

Beast Market

Market Place Wall

Pigs Sheep Cattle Horses

Timber Joinery

1308 -The Shambles - butchers meat and spices sold

1726 - Exchange Buildings

1929 - New Council House

Butter Cross

Hen Cross

The Poultry

Site of various fairs attracting traders from far afield
1155 - Charter confirms Saturday market
1284 - Nottingham Fair mentioned
1542 - Goose Fair first mentioned by name

Markets and Fairs

Unlike Newark, York or Shrewsbury, Nottingham's centre is bereft of medieval buildings and has just one former coaching inn, the Flying Horse, which is now an arcade. The square's importance, like the castle's, is due to its site. Since Norman times, it has been the venue for a weekly market, and also for a yearly fair, later known as Goose Fair. Together with the larger Lenton Fair, they lasted for many days and were vital for town and country folk alike to sell wares and purchase them from all areas of the known world.

However, as a natural meeting point, it has been witness to many great moments in the county's history. Just like other well-known squares, its importance is due to historical connections. St Petersburg's Square was the setting for the October 1917 Revolution when the Bolsheviks surrounded the Winter Palace and took over control of the government. Thus began the era of Soviet communism. Paris's Place de la Concorde was the setting for the guillotine during France's turbulent revolution. Thousands fell victim to its blade during 1793-94.

All squares will have their stories of important events. One of Nottingham's was the civic reception for the Nottingham Forest team after their European Cup win in 1979. But two other occasions from the past highlight its importance as the meeting point for the county.

Glorious Revolution

In 1688 the square became a focal point in the revolt against King James II. James, wanting to steer the country back towards Catholicism, repealed the laws preventing Catholics from holding high office and began to appoint them to positions of influence. When his wife gave birth to a son and heir, the Protestants feared a Catholic succession. They invited William of Orange, husband of James's daughter Mary, to invade England with their support. The plot called for William Cavendish, Earl of Devonshire, to seize Nottingham. He did so easily and was soon joined by Lord Delamere and Sir Scrope Howe with their regiments of mounted horsemen. On market day, Saturday 24 November, Cavendish, Delamere and Howe addressed the people at the Malt Cross, in the square, and explained why they were supporting a coup. They soon had the crowd cheering them on.

On 2 December, James II's youngest daughter rode to Nottingham to join the conspirators and, by doing so, added legitimacy to their campaign. As the Prince of Orange began his advance on London, support for James collapsed. He fled to France and William became William III of England.

Riots

In March 1831 a great crowd gathered in the square to hear talk about the Reform Bill. The Bill aimed to increase the number of citizens eligible to vote and to end anomalies such as that in Retford, which had two MPs, while much larger towns, such as flourishing Manchester, had none. The working classes saw it as a vital step forward in an age of industrial unrest and unemployment, and signed a petition in support. On Monday 10 October the same year, 20,000 people crowded into the square for another reform rally after the House of Lords had rejected the Bill. Feelings ran high in the town, packed with visitors to Goose Fair. Shops were looted and some of the crowd attacked houses known to belong to opponents of the Bill, while others tried to break open the prisons. On Monday afternoon order broke down: a windmill in the forest (belonging to an anti-reformer) was attacked, Colwick Hall was pillaged, and around 600 rioters rushed to the site of Nottingham Castle and set fire to the Duke of Newcastle's mansion. It burnt to a shell.

Market Square in 1861. (Courtesy of Picture the Past, NTGM009111)

The following day the rioting continued. William Low's silk mill in Beeston was set on fire, Lenton Hall was plundered and the mob attempted, but failed, to sack Wollaton Hall. Several prisoners were taken and escorted through the Market Square to the jail. There were also riots in Derby, Bristol and Worcester and huge public meetings all over the country. The following January, three prisoners were hanged but, denied reform for far too long, they had made their point. In 1832 the Lords finally passed the Bill, but only after King William IV, under pressure from his Prime Minister, threatened to create at least fifty new peers.

Viewing

Open every day. The on-site visitor centre (0115 9155330) can book you on various tours that include the square and will point out buildings worthy of note, such as Bromley House (the best surviving example of a Georgian house, built 1752) and the Bell Inn, both on Angel Row.

NOTTINGHAM'S CAVES

This entry is well covered by two local history booklets: 'Nottingham City of Caves' by Andrew Hamilton, which is short, well-illustrated and with a comprehensive map, and 'Sandstone Caves of Nottingham' by Tony Waltham (revised 2008) with more detail and also excellent diagrams and maps. Both reveal the incredible number of caves that the city plays host to, making the statement 'Nottingham has more man-made caves than any other city in Britain' seem almost obvious.

The phrase 'man-made' is the key factor here. Most caves form naturally through the action of acids in groundwater dissolving softer rocks such as limestone and dolomite. Most of Turkey's 40,000 caves and the caves of southern Spain are of this type, as are the Derbyshire caves, including Creswell Crags. Some caves, however, have been dug out by humans, such as those of the village of Matmata in Tunisia, where the Berber people have worked the soft carboniferous shale into dwellings for hundreds of years. All Nottingham's caves were also hewn, but from sandstone, soft enough to be dug out, yet hard and stable enough to build on. The sandstone plateau, formed over 60 million years ago, stretches all the way up to Mansfield, which also has a cave or two.

Basic Facts

Nottingham's surface caves, those hollowed out above ground level, were probably used as dwelling places and could have been built during the Saxon period or earlier. Perhaps some were in use before the Romans came in the first century AD, hacked out by the Celts. Exact dates are not known. The earliest reference to the caves was in AD 868 when Asser, a ninth-century monk historian, referred to them. However he gave no details, and the next direct references are the Borough records, which indicate increasing use from the thirteenth to eighteenth centuries. We know that these were mostly cellar caves because they have survived in great number. We also know they were used for a variety of purposes, including the storage of foodstuffs and wool; as areas where brewing, tanning and malting took place; and where wells were bored for fresh water. The constant, cool temperature of a basement or cellar cave is an ideal place for the storage of grain and wool, and fish from the local River Leen. It was also ideal for malting barley, and for storing the ale that it produced. Nottingham was well-known for its brewing from the thirteenth century and in 1641, there were sixty maltsters living in the town.

Broad Marsh Caves.

As the town grew after the establishment of the Norman castle, more tradespeople were needed and more caves were constructed. Maps show that they tend to relate to the boundaries of the properties on the surface and hence it is fairly safe to assume they date from the period when the medieval street plan was established.

Asser was a Welsh monk who became Bishop of Sherborne in the 890s. His biography of King Alfred enables us to know more about this King than any other King in the Dark Ages. Yet, like so many priceless books of antiquity, it was nearly lost to the world when it was kept in the Cotton Library. Sir Robert Cotton (1571-1631) amassed one of the greatest collections of Old and Middle English books in the country, but a quarter were destroyed or damaged by a fire in 1731, including the only copy of Asser's book in existence. Luckily, various parts of his book had been copied elsewhere, and the work has been reconstructed.

Visiting

Most of the surface caves used as dwelling places have been destroyed, although some can still be seen around the castle rock. Some of the caves on view at Broad Marsh City of Caves (0115 9881955) were built into the rockface and had views over the Trent Valley. Today they are blocked in for security reasons and you have to imagine the view, but this is still an impressive site. In the cellar caves you can see a roomful of tanning pits, wells and plenty of passageways with nooks and crannies.

A cave tour, including Mortimer's Hole, can be booked at the castle. The Bell Inn is happy to arrange a tour of its cellars (telephone 0115 9475241 to book). The Salutation Inn will allow trips to their cellars if asked. Guided tours are available for the caves at the Shire Hall (Galleries of Justice), under Wollaton Hall and behind the Brewhouse Yard.

Perhaps the most fascinating is The Park tunnel, quarried by the noted architect, T.C. Hine, through the rock in 1856 as an entranceway into the developing, exclusive Park estate (enter via Tunnel Road in The Park).

OLLERTON WATERMILL

Of the 9,250 manors investigated by the Domesday Survey, around a third (3,463) had 5,624 mills between them. All were watermills for grinding corn. The water turned the paddle wheel, made of elm or oak, which turned the millstone via an axle and a system of interlocking cogwheels. If the water driving the wheel was too shallow or too slow, a millpond was made by damming the stream just above the mill, allowing water to be fed to the mill through a system of sluices.

The windmill and the fulling mill did not make their appearance in England until the end of the twelfth century. From then until the invention of the steam engine in the eighteenth century, water, wind and animal muscle were the sole sources of mechanical power.

Ollerton Mill, the only working watermill in Nottinghamshire, is on a site where the river can still flow fast and high. It was built in 1713, almost certainly on a Saxon site (Domesday listed three mills for Ollerton). Once a site had been selected and a stream diverted or dammed, it would tend to continue in use. This mill worked commercially until 1984 and was

Ollerton Watermill.

restored in 1993 by a family whose ancestors have been milling since the seventeenth century. The mill is across the road from two old coaching inns, the Hop Pole and the White Hart. The village used to be a route centre, the crossing point of the York-London, Worksop-Newark and Lincoln-Mansfield roads. Ollerton's mill stands as if untouched by time, a place where one can experience something that was vital to the medieval economy.

Corn

The watermill appeared in England around the eighth century (Wellington Mill, Herefordshire, is dated at AD 696) and spread steadily over eastern England and the Midlands during the next 300 years. They were less abundant in the west and north as the ancient method using two round stones, known as the hand-quern, was still practised.

Grain was ground into flour and used to make the coarse, flat bread of the day. This, along with vegetables, would have constituted the peasant's staple diet. The tenants of the manor would have been forced to use their local mill and obliged to give the miller a 10 per cent cut, either by way of produce or, as the money economy developed (especially after the Black Death), in coins.

Because the streams and rivers were not always a reliable source of power, windmills were introduced. The earliest windmills are recorded in the reign of Richard I (1272-1307), after which they spread rapidly, especially in southern and eastern England.

Cloth

In the early Middle Ages cloth was woven in England, but little was for export. It was not good enough, but our raw wool was. The wool was exported to the looms of Flanders and Italy and brought in a certain amount of wealth to the merchants and the King. In the fourteenth century a great change began. Edward III (1327-77) introduced Flemish weavers into the country and helped protect them. Their skills gradually spread over the country and England became a cloth exporter, which was much more lucrative than exporting raw wool. Cloth soon became England's chief source of wealth and merchants became wealthy enough to fund chantries (see Newark St Mary's). Trains of packhorses carried bales of cloth to the coast, and merchants busied themselves finding markets in the Baltic and the Levant, and later in the American colonies.

Watermills played their part in the rise of the woollen cloth industry in the late Middle Ages, being used in the fulling process. The water power drove a frame of pounding hammers that compressed the fibres, binding them together, thereby strengthening the freshly-woven cloth (previously cloth had been fulled by people treading it barefoot). The broadcloth produced became England's major export in the fourteenth and fifteenth centuries. In the area around the mills, many small rural trades grew up to service the industry, such as carders (men who combed the wool), staplers (people who graded and sold the wool), spinners and weavers, among others.

At the end of the seventeenth century there were probably over 20,000 watermills in England, and by then, paper, leather and even gunpowder were benefiting from the use of waterpower.

Fall and Rise Again?

Both watermills and windmills became old technology in the nineteenth century. Steam-powered factories with steel rollers were far more efficient. By the end of the twentieth century only a few mills were still operating, most of them heritage sites. According to the

Society for the Protection of Ancient Buildings, there were less than sixty mills in the UK working commercially in 1997. At the start of the century there had been 15,000.

The Department of Trade and Industry has recently introduced an initiative that may bring some of the derelict mills back into production. Under their Clear Skies scheme, grants of several thousand pounds are available to mill owners to enable them to renovate their equipment and install generators to supply 'green power' to the National Grid. Traditionally the mill's mechanics are low-maintenance and should last about twenty-five years. Depending on the reliability and the rate of the flow of water, both the mill owners and the country could benefit.

Visiting

The three-storey building, with information boards and audio-visual display, is a delight to visit. Well preserved, it is complete with hoppers, sack-hoists and grindstones. The watermill is in operation from April to September, Sunday afternoons and Bank Holidays, 12 p.m.–5 p.m., subject to a small charge. Group visits welcome at other times by arrangement (01623 822469). The excellent teashop is open Wednesday–Sunday, 10.30 a.m.–4 p.m.

PAPPLEWICK PUMPING STATION

Papplewick Pumping Station is a spectacular example of Victorian architecture, the ornate brickwork and carved stone being typical of the period. Inside, the pillars are richly decorated and the beautiful stained-glass windows reflect a water theme. It claims to be the finest working Victorian water-pumping station in Britain and still runs the two original James Watt & Co. single-cylinder rotative engines installed in 1884. The building is set in beautifully landscaped gardens with an ornamental cooling pond and fountain. The whole site demonstrates both the skill and technical expertise of the Victorian engineers and also the priority given to the supply of fresh water in the second half of the nineteenth century. The priority was born of necessity. Cholera threatened the country and pumping stations played a crucial role in the fight against it. Also, two Nottingham engineers played an important role in the development of these stations.

Fresh Water

In the nineteenth century, Nottingham had a problem – fresh water, or, more precisely, the lack of it. In previous centuries the county towns had plenty of clean water, hand-pumped from wells drawing water from the springs that fed the various rivers. The Trent served Newark, the Leen served Nottingham, the Maun served Mansfield and the Idle served Retford. Until late in the eighteenth century, this was sufficient. Then the Industrial Revolution brought huge numbers of people from the countryside to fast-industrializing cities and towns. The poor ended up in overcrowded slums with narrow streets and no washing facilities; rubbish was dumped in the streets and often accumulated into stinking piles; and sewage was discharged into the very rivers from which they drew their drinking water. Death rates from bacterial diseases such as typhoid, spread by contaminated water and food, were high, yet many people refused to make the link between disease and the water supply.

Papplewick Pumping Station.

Cholera

In 1831 the problems were compounded by the arrival in Britain of a deadly new disease – cholera. Germs from contaminated water invading the bowels led to fluid loss and death by dehydration. It had been a killer in Asia for 1,000 years and spread to Europe in 1817. The 1831 visitation, however, was particularly virulent. It started in India at the Kumbh Festival on the River Ganges. When people returned to their villages, they took the infection with them. Thousands died, including 10,000 British troops. It then raged along the trade routes to Iran, Baku, Astrakhan and up the Volga to Russia, in time for the autumn Festival of Nijni-Novgorod. Visiting merchants took it back with them to Europe, and in late 1831 it arrived in Sunderland via steamship. 32,000 died in Britain and millions worldwide.

In 1838 a bad outbreak of fever in London led to a Poor Law Enquiry, whose comments on disease and the water supply shocked the public. In 1848 another cholera outbreak led to 70,000 deaths.

Finally, in 1854, Dr John Snow made a breakthrough. A sudden outbreak of cholera occurred in London, killing 127 people in three days, all living in or around Broad Street. Snow traced the infection to one pump and, after it was closed down, the epidemic ceased. At first many refused to believe the obvious connection, but the idea became accepted that the disease was spread by contaminated water, especially after Louis Pasteur proved that specific diseases were caused by specific microbes.

More deaths from cholera came in 1857 (30,000) and 1866 (18,000). In 1869, a Royal Commission recommended good water supply and sewage disposal, but it was not until 1875 that the big breakthrough came. Local authorities were made responsible for lighting, water supplies, sewage, parks, toilets and housing. The towns had to act. Pumping stations, already well-established, were now built throughout the country, and, as most towns had experienced prosperity from industrial growth, they built them to impress.

Nottingham's Example

Nottingham was a typical example. In 1696 the first Nottingham Waterworks took water from the Leen to a small reservoir on Park Row, from where it was piped to various parts of the town. As demand increased, more water supply companies were set up, and the engineer of one of them was Thomas Hawksley. He designed the Trent Bridge Waterworks in 1831, taking water from the Trent, filtering it, and pumping it under pressure to street taps. It was Britain's first high-pressure 'constant supply', preventing contamination entering the supply of clean water mains. By 1845 there were three companies. They amalgamated and the new company built three new pumping stations – at the Ropewalk, Haydn Road, Basford, and Bestwood Park, all extracting water from the sandstone beds underneath Nottingham. (Bestwood's building still exists on the A60, but is now a health spa and restaurant.)

In 1880 the Nottingham Corporation took control and their chief engineer, Ogle Tarbotton, advised that the needs of the ever-growing population demanded another new station. The city, riding on the success of the lace and other industries, saw an opportunity to flaunt its prosperity. Papplewick was born in 1884 and, as a result, all the other works became redundant.

Thomas Hawksley was born at Arnold, Nottingham, in 1807. His success led him to be appointed to oversee water supply projects in towns throughout Britain, including Liverpool, Leeds, Sheffield, Leicester and Derby. He was elected President of the Institute of Civil Engineers in 1872 and also received knighthoods and other honours from Brazil, Sweden, Denmark and other countries for helping with their water distribution problems.

Marriot Ogle Tarbotton was the first municipal engineer in the world to employ subways under streets to carry public services, such as gas, sewers, etc. He built University College in Shakespeare Street and laid the foundations for the present inner city boulevards. He is best known though for replacing the old bridge over the River Trent with the structure that stands today.

Nowadays

In 1899, Nottingham joined with Derby, Leicester and Sheffield to extract water from new reservoirs at Howden, Derwent and Ladybower. The water ran from these to mix with the Papplewick water before entering the system.

In the 1990s, Carsington Reservoir was built to supply Nottingham, taking water from the River Derwent in the winter and releasing it back during the summer.

Visiting

Papplewick was electrified in 1969 but can still use the steam engines, and does so on open days.

Open Sunday afternoons and in-steam on Bank Holidays and selected weekends throughout the year. It is an excellent place to visit (0115 9632938).

RUDDINGTON FRAMEWORK KNITTERS MUSEUM

This is more than a museum, occupying an actual domestic factory site established in 1829, when there were around 280 houses in Ruddington with framework knitting machines. By 1841 the number had risen to 387, and by 1861 to 515. In 1844 there were 16,382 frames in Nottinghamshire. This county was the home of framework knitting machines which made knitted silk, woollen and, later, cotton stockings.

During the sixteenth century there was a change in fashion for men towards wearing knee-length breeches with long stockings (a fashion lasting 250 years!). William Lee, possibly from Calverton and aware of the profits to be made from increased production, invented the stocking frame in 1589. During the seventeenth and eighteenth centuries, his frame was adapted and improved so that, by 1850, the East Midlands had over 100,000 people working in the framework knitting industry producing hosiery. Lee's invention was the first of the major textile inventions which originated in Britain. These inventions were crucial to the Industrial Revolution that propelled Britain, for a time during the nineteenth century, to the top of the leaderboard of the world's most influential countries. This site is second only to the Lace Market as a link to the Industrial Revolution.

Framework knitting machines at Ruddington.

Stocking Frame

William Lee's stocking frame, made up of 2,000 individual parts powered by a foot pedal, was far more sophisticated than the later and more well-known inventions of Arkwright, Cartwright and Crompton. Failing to gain a patent in England, he took his machines to France where they were used to help set up a silk knitting industry. They re-emerged in London where, despite there being less than 100 machines by the 1660s, their use became regulated by the Handwork Knitters Association. To avoid their restrictive practices and to take advantage of cheaper labour in the provinces, machine operators began to move to the East Midlands. Henceforth, it was this region that dominated the trade.

Date	East Midlands	UK
1660	100	1,000
1720	3,000	8,000
1800	22,000	24,000

Estimated number of knitting frames.

During the second half of the eighteenth century, adaptations were made to the machines enabling them to produce a greater variety of goods, such as wider pieces of fabric with patterns, gloves, shawls and other garments.

Organisation

Framework knitting was village-based early on because workers could combine the trade with agricultural work. However, it soon became a full-time trade involving whole families. While husbands and older males operated the frames, the women would wind the yarn on to the frame's bobbins or 'finish' the hose with embroidery or other needlework. From the early days, the knitters had to rely on middlemen who supplied them with the yarn and purchased their finished product. They, in turn, made their profit by selling on, at a higher price, to a master hosier who marketed the product. The middlemen's control over the knitters increased when they purchased the frames, which the knitters had to rent from them. This was a profitable move for the middlemen because, although the frames were expensive, they made their money back within a few years from the rents they charged. Meanwhile, the machines would last for twenty years or more, bringing in profit. When demand fell it was the knitters who suffered. They had to pay their rent and pay for their yarn whether they could sell their cloth or not.

The advantages of the domestic organisation of the trade were so great for the middlemen that there was little incentive to introduce steam power – the labour costs were cheap enough. There was, however, a movement towards grouping machines together in 'frameshops' where the middlemen could charge a rent for the space. To make any money, the knitters had to work long hours and, with candles being expensive, these frameshops were built with long rows of large windows to take maximum use of any natural light. Machines were also crammed together to use all the space. Ruddington's frameshop still has machines packed together, in working order, which can be demonstrated to visitors.

Influence

This trade played a huge part in industrial growth both locally and nationally. In the second half of the nineteenth century, as foot-propelled frames were replaced by powered machines in large factories, the domestic industry declined. However, continual adaptation of the mechanics of the machine eventually produced the lace machines crucial to the development of Nottinghamshire's industry.

In the second half of the eighteenth century, when demand for hosiery was growing, the trade placed extra demands on the spinners of yarn, especially cotton yarn. These demands led to the inventions of James Hargreaves' spinning jenny and Richard Arkwright's water frame and others crucial to the Industrial Revolution. Lee's invention had shown what was possible a century before! With the main demand coming from the Lancashire cotton weavers, imports of raw cotton spiralled from a little over 1,000 tons of cotton a year in 1760 to over 222,000 tons by 1850. For a period after 1850, Britain produced more than two-thirds of the world's coal and more than half of the world's iron and cloth. Britain was the 'workshop of the world' and had the highest per capita income in the world.

But remember, the stocking frame, there at the start, is on display at Ruddington.

Visiting

This is the only surviving example of a nineteenth-century knitter's yard, with workshops arranged around a garden courtyard. It is full of fascinating information about framework knitting, Luddites and much more. Contact for details of times and charges (0115 9846914). You can even try your hand at knitting at this excellent museum, where there is also a shop and refreshments.

RUFFORD ABBEY

The priories of Blyth and Worksop illustrate the monastery story, so why see Rufford? Firstly, because monasteries were so influential to the medieval community, but secondly because it is a superb example of a modern-day heritage site, designed to meet the needs of today's tourist industry.

This has all the requisite items for a modern day out: some remains of a twelfth-century monastery, even more remains of a grand country house, a large area of parkland with walks, gardens and lake, a craft centre, a gallery, several seventeenth-century ice-houses, a coffee shop and a restaurant. You can purchase an inexpensive booklet, 'Rufford Past & Present', which has excellent detail about the site and its monastic history. There is also an exhibition which traces the history of the Cistercian monks from the twelfth century to the Dissolution of the Monasteries.

This place is an example of history of another kind – the history of tourism itself. As Nottinghamshire encountered the decline of its basic industries in the twentieth century – Raleigh cycles, textile manufacturing and coal mining, among others – so it had to face up to the necessity of change. Along with other areas of the country, it began to promote its heritage; its history. Using Robin Hood as its spearhead, the county has helped to develop many attractions, of which Rufford is almost a symbol.

Above: Rufford
Abbey.

Left: Rufford Abbey
cellar.

The Change

In the Middle Ages, the majority of the population were tied to their local communities, unable even to travel without their lord's permission. During the Industrial Revolution, the majority of the population moved to the towns or their suburbs. Incomes rose, days off increased and the railways brought cheap travel. By the late nineteenth century, the working classes began to travel to the seaside. Blackpool, Brighton, Bournemouth and other towns changed to accommodate them. In the 1960s came the jet aeroplane and the start of the annual migration abroad.

However there has been another change in habits, which has been just as fundamental. In the Middle Ages, religion acted as the focus for the greater part of society. In a world where much was still unknown, religion's history and values were shared by the community. With the decline in active religious participation there has been a corresponding increase in a search for identity. Increasingly people are looking for their roots in history – of their society and of their family. The search for one's family tree has been a direct result of this change. A desire to know more about the history of one's local area and one's country is another change that is now ongoing.

Heritage Explosion

During the twentieth century, Britain changed from an economy based on industrial manufacturing to one based on services. Coal mining, steel production and shipbuilding were among the industries that declined drastically, causing hardship to the communities where they were based. Even car production, a twentieth-century industry, shrank considerably. At the same time, tourism began to rise. Since the 1970s, Britain has remarketed itself as a heritage destination to capitalise on the desire for more holidays and short breaks. In 2002-03, British tourist revenue was £75 billion, of which £60 billion was spent by domestic tourists. Heritage sites have increased considerably in number, as evidenced by the profusion of brown signposts.

Specific places to visit began to appear from the late nineteenth century as a result of a number of measures designed to preserve Britain's heritage:

- 1882 – Ancient Monuments Protection Act. Buildings were listed.

- 1895 – National Trust founded. It is now the biggest conservation body in Europe with a membership of over 3.4 million.

- 1949 – National Parks established. The Peak District (1951) was the first of fourteen parks in the UK.

- 1983 – English Heritage established. Part government-funded, it works with local authorities and other bodies to promote and conserve the historic environment.

Another route to conservation was, strangely enough, the introduction of death duties in 1894. Many owners could not afford to keep their large houses in repair. Between 1918 and 1945, 485 houses were demolished. Others responded by opening to the public, for example, Longleat (1949), Beaulieu (1952) and Woburn Abbey (1955). Rufford was one of a large number of houses that were requisitioned by the government at the outbreak of the war in 1939 to be used as training establishments and hospitals and the like. It had been converted to a country house following the Dissolution of the Monasteries, and remained so until 1938. Faced by rising taxes and wages, the estate was then sold privately. It emerged after the war in a poor state of repair and, in 1952 ,was eventually purchased by Nottinghamshire County Council who designated it as a country park in 1969. With funding from English Heritage, an improvement programme began, including a £55,000 restoration of the lake and the planting of 10,000 trees.

The heritage industry has had a huge boost from the National Lottery. Grants from this source totalled £209 million in 2005-06 out of a total expenditure of £321 million. Recent National Lottery projects include:

- The National Football Museum, Preston – £14 million.

- Renaissance of Cotswold Canals – £27 million.

- Chatham Historic Dockyard – £17 million.

- Bestwood Engine Winding House – £907,000.

- Wollaton Hall – £4.5 million.

Another recent source of funding is the European Regional Development Fund, which recently put £7 million into Wollaton Park and £252,000 into restoring the Chesterfield Canal.

Other Sites
Wollaton Hall, the D.H. Lawrence Museum and the Southwell Workhouse are all classic heritage sites.

Mr Straw's House – a small, semi-detached, Edwardian house, preserved because it remained unaltered until the National Trust took possession in 1990. A good example of how the nation is using its heritage as an attraction.

Popular History!
Some argue there is a danger that people looking to experience history may end up merely seeing a selection of entertainment sites. On the other hand, it would be wrong to condemn all attempts to popularise history. Sites such as the Jorvik Viking Centre may portray an idealised past, but they could inspire people to want to know more. Not everyone wants to spend hours poring over museum exhibits. If we can all learn enough to put the present into context, to realise that history can be interpreted in different ways and to see history's recurring themes and cycles, it will be worthwhile.

Visiting
Open every day (01623 822944).

SHERWOOD FOREST

Famous in England and throughout the world as the home of the notorious outlaw Robin Hood, visitors will come hoping to see an impenetrable medieval forest with deer flitting through the occasional leafy glade. The Major Oak will also be on everyone's must-see list, the venerable tree amongst whose branches Robin is reputed to have lain, concealed from wealthy travellers.

A forest oak – not the Major.

What is the reality? Robin and his Merrie Men disappeared over 700 years ago, so the chances of meeting them now are pretty slim! According to Professor Holt (one-time Professor of Medieval History at the University of Cambridge) in his well-researched and readable book *Robin Hood*, 'It is more likely than not that Robert Hood, outlaw, the original of the story, was a real person'. He also details enough evidence to be able to state 'that tales of Robin were sufficiently well-known by 1296'. So, given that the tale would have taken years to develop into a regular story passed around by travelling bards, it is possible that Robin was shooting his arrows during the reign of Richard the Lionheart (1189-99).

What about the Major Oak? That exists, and very impressive it is too. It was brought to fame by antiquarian Major Hayman Rooke, who described it in his 1790 book *Remarkable Oaks in the Park of Welbeck*. Thought to be at least 800 years old, did Robin ever lay against it thinking of Maid Marion? We don't know, but it was almost certainly around in his day.

And the forest? In Robin's day it would have covered an area of around 100,000 acres, stretching from Arnold to Worksop, with many dense patches of oak and beech trees amongst which outlaws could hide. Wolves and wild boar would also have lurked there, although they were becoming scarce by the twelfth century. However, much of the area known as Sherwood Forest will have been less thickly wooded and have contained some heath and grassland, ideal for deer and other game. Also included in the forest were various settlements such as Mansfield, Papplewick and Blidworth, and the twelfth-century priories of Worksop, Rufford, Welbeck and Newstead, all with large, cleared areas for agricultural use.

The ruins of Clipstone Palace.

Today there is still a forest, despite 80 per cent of the forest's oaks being cut down for shipbuilding and housing during the period 1600-1790. The area of the country park is now only 450 acres; however, there are still more than 900 oak trees over 600 years old. This makes it one of the largest areas of ancient oaks in the world. Other areas of Sherwood Forest also still exist. Sherwood Pines Forest Park, between Old Clipstone and Ollerton (nearly 3,000 acres), has the largest area of woodland open to the public in the East Midlands, a visitor centre and hiking trails. Up to 1,500 of the 3,800 acres of Clumber Park are still woodland. Haywood Oaks, near Blidworth, is a small forest with mature oak trees several hundred years old. Add in the wooded areas of Blidworth Woods, Harlow Woods, Thieves Wood, Rufford Park and Newstead Abbey, and we arrive at around 6,000 acres of forest. It is certainly enough for anyone with imagination to travel to the days when the narrow, main road between London and York wound its way through the trees at the edge of the forest. In the twelfth and thirteenth centuries, travellers would have ensured some armed, fellow travellers or guards accompanied them, it being a well-known haunt of robbers and thieves. Now you can roam in freedom or follow well-signposted walks.

Nottinghamshire or Yorkshire?

Many of the early stories revolve around Barnsdale, near Wakefield, Yorkshire, on the Great North Road. However, there is no forest there, but then not all the early stories were centred on a forest. Many were though, and Sherwood was only thirty miles away, so Robin and his band could easily have moved between the two to evade pursuit and capture. Sherwood was a well-known haunt of outlaws by the end of the twelfth century, and a plausible and likely setting for the activities of Robin Hood.

Forest Laws

The Danish and Saxon kings loved to hunt the deer and wild boar in the huge forests, while the local people could forage for timber and hunt rabbits and hares. But use of the Forest's resources was gradually restricted. King Cnut imposed fines on poachers and Edward the Confessor had forest wardens, but after 1066, when the Normans took over, large areas of land were deemed

Royal Forest, where only the King and his retinue could hunt. By the middle of the twelfth century, as much as a third of England, from the Forest of Northumberland in the north-east to Dartmoor in the south-west, was subject to Forest Law. The laws were enforced at special courts and penalties for poaching, foraging and even carrying a bow and arrow in the forest could be severe, including blinding, castration and mutilation. Not until 1217 were the harsh laws abolished in favour of fines and imprisonment, which shows how seriously the sport of hunting was taken.

Other Sites Associated With Robin Hood

- Edwinstowe Church, where Robin married Maid Marion, was a sixteenth-century addition to the story. The church dates from around 1175.

- Rufford Abbey, where Robin formed his band of Merrie Men, was founded in 1146, so would have been there when Robin was around.

- Robin Hood's Well, etc. Professor Holt's comments are well worth quoting here: 'No evidence at all that Robin Hood ever took ship in his "bay", or sat in any of his several "chairs", or leapt his "leaps", or hid in his "cave", or used his "stables", or drank from his many "wells"'. It would have been useful for storytellers to find local examples to add realism to their tale, and the local innkeepers wouldn't have objected.

- Clipstone Palace was built in the reign of Henry II (1154–89). It was a hunting lodge in full splendour by the end of the twelfth century, Robin's likely era. The medieval English kings loved to hunt and many of them stayed here, including Henry II, Richard Lionheart, John, Henry III and Edwards I, II and III. They needed to be big to accommodate members of the King's court and his small private army. Excavations and a geophysical survey have revealed a large group of buildings that would have consisted of a Great Hall, Knight's Hall, Queen's Hall, Great Chapel, Great Chamber, kitchen, King's Kitchen, Treasurer's Chamber, pantry, buttery and stabling for 200 horses. Today, like Lenton Abbey, there are only scant remains. (Take the B6030 through Old Clipstone towards Mansfield and park in the lay-by just outside the village. Walk back 200 metres and the ruins are in view in a private field. Please view from a safe distance.)

Visiting

There is a good visitor centre with restaurant/snack bar. Telephone for opening hours (01623 823202). Forest walks open daily.

SHIRE HALL

The current building on this site was built in 1770. It now houses the Galleries of Justice Museum, an excellent attraction where you can experience the atmosphere of 300 years of crime and punishment and witness a 'real trial' in the authentic Victorian courtroom (for which the museum has won a number of awards). The chances are you will be found guilty and ushered to meet the prison warders, who will decide your fate. Be prepared to be sentenced and 'sent down' to the original cells and maze of medieval caves. These help ensure that this is more than an attraction – it is also a genuine historical site with links to over 1,000 years of history. Going back to the eighth century when the shires first began to evolve in the south of the country, the King's representative would have been the ealdorman (later known as the earl). He was responsible for collecting taxes and ensuring that justice was upheld within his shire. Later, when these ealdormen were given the prestige and responsibility of governing several shires, a shire-reeve (sheriff) was appointed to manage each one. As the shire system gradually extended throughout England in the tenth and eleventh centuries, the sheriff began to take on the responsibility of local government. He presided over the shire court, ran the gaol for prisoners awaiting trial and organised executions.

A sheriff's court for Nottinghamshire and Derbyshire appears to have sat in St James' Chapel, part of the Carmelite Friary on St James' Street in early Norman times. Perhaps the castle's dungeons were used as the prison. Before then the court would probably have been sited within the old Anglian burgh, perhaps
close to the current site. There are references to the presence of the Shire Hall on High Pavement in 1375. However, as there are no deeds to the Shire Hall because it did not experience a change of ownership until the 1980s, this spot could well have been the site for much longer. The position is right, inside the Anglian burgh, opposite St Mary's Church, and just down the road from the Weekday (market) cross.

In the fifteenth and sixteenth centuries, the Shire Hall was the meeting place where Knights of the Shire were selected to serve the county in Parliament. In 1567 the practice of sharing a sheriff with Derbyshire ceased. Henceforth, Nottinghamshire had its very own.

The Sheriff

The sheriff, being in a position to make a lot of money, became a very important man. He could arrange with the King to pay a fixed yearly sum, which he would collect in the form of taxes, fines, duties, etc. He was then able to pocket the difference between what he collected and what he paid to the King. He tended therefore to be distrusted and his unpopularity was reflected in the tales of Robin Hood. Because of this, the towns were keen to be free of the sheriff's influence and sought charters to run their own affairs. Nottingham was granted the status of a county in its own right in 1449, an important step towards becoming independent.

Another factor in the demise of the sheriff was the introduction of Justices of the Peace in the fourteenth century. These were picked by the King to administer justice at the Quarter Sessions (held four times a year at the Shire Hall), formerly the sheriff's job.

Change of Use

The population of the county of Nottinghamshire and its city increased considerably in the nineteenth century. More administrators were needed to provide education, roads, healthcare, housing and leisure facilities, as well as police and a penal service. Both the Shire Hall and the Guild Hall (Nottingham's Town Hall, dated to at least the thirteenth century, where the town's debtors and felons were tried and gaoled), along the street from the Shire Hall, were too small. New ones were needed. In 1888 a new Guild Hall was built for the City Council in Burton Street, and in 1894 the old building was demolished to make way for a railway line. Around the same time, in 1877, the Shire Hall was restored with the front being redesigned by

Shire Hall.

the prestigious architect, T.C. Hine (note the misspelling of the word gaol on the stonework) but it was still too small. When the new Council House was erected in the square in 1929, the County Council were able to use some of its facilities. However, much larger premises were needed and in 1935 a site was purchased adjoining Trent Bridge. The County Council building, the new Shire Hall, was finally completed in 1965.

The old building became redundant, but was protected by being part of the Lace Market heritage site. After several years of neglect, it became a tourist/heritage attraction. There are far worse fates. With the decline of organised religion and with families' relatives scattered all over the country, people are delving into the past researching their family history as a means of finding out where they belong in the community. This in turn helps to make local and national history more relevant.

Other similar examples include Bodmin's Shire Hall (used as the county court until 1988), Dorchester's Grade I listed Shire Hall (built 1797, and where the Tolpuddle Martyrs were sentenced to seven years' transportation for trying to establish a trade union), and Monmouth's Shire Hall (where chartists were sentenced to be 'hung, drawn and quartered' in 1839), which are all now crime and punishment attractions.

Sheriffs of the Wild West

Today there are only sixteen sheriffs in the whole of England and Wales. However, there are over 3,000 in the United States of America doing the same job as the sheriffs used to do in England. The former American colonies obtained their independence from England in 1776 and based their legal system on the English one at that time. It was not until 1829 that the sheriff handed over his vital law enforcement role to the new police force set up by Prime Minister Robert Peel.

Visiting

Best viewed in conjunction with the Broad Marsh Caves, there is a joint ticket available. Open all year, telephone for details (0115 9520555).

SOUTHWELL MINSTER

A truly impressive building in a lovely setting, it compares well with the likes of Westminster and Winchester Cathedrals. The distinctive pyramidal spires of lead (or pepperpot spires as they are known locally), are the only example of their kind in the UK. This picture shows the grand building slowly being lit up by the sun, a reflection of the time when it was built. Northern Europe was emerging from the Dark Ages, and stone buildings were replacing wooden ones, but the Reformation (the rebirth of learning) had yet to make a big impact. Europeans were still ignorant of the Americas and the Pacific, still hazy about the locations of India and China, and the common people thought the world was flat.

The Minster is Born

A minster is a church run by priests who worked and preached in the surrounding villages. In Anglo-Saxon times many such churches were attached to monasteries, for example, York and Canterbury. It didn't mean they were monasteries themselves. Southwell was not a monastery and it became a cathedral (chief church in an administrative area or diocese) in 1884 when a bishop was appointed.

It is probable that a church existed on the Southwell site by AD 660, possibly founded by Paulinus, the first Bishop of York, in AD 627 while on a visit to the area to baptise believers in the River Trent. The window nearest to the font shows Paulinus holding a model of the minster, the blue line said to represent the Trent. Southwell was of sufficent importance for the Abbess of Repton to be buried there in the seventh century (according to a document of 1014). We also know that in AD 956 King Eadwig gave a gift of land to Oscytel, the Danish Archbishop of York, on which a minster church was established. In 1108, the project of rebuilding the Saxon church at Southwell to become a large Norman church began.

Between 1050 and 1350 was the great age of building churches and cathedrals in Europe. During these three centuries, several million tons of stone were quarried in France for the building of eighty cathedrals, 500 large churches and some tens of thousands of parish churches around Europe. Among the English cathedrals were Canterbury, Durham, Ely, Exeter, Lincoln, Peterborough, Salisbury, Westminster Abbey and Wells. The European ones include Chartres, Paris-Notre-Dame, Cologne, Pisa, Siena and Santiago de Compostela. According to Jean Gimpel in *The Cathedral Builders*, more stone was excavated in France in these three centuries than at any time in ancient Egypt.

Southwell Minster.

Why Build Then?

The Vikings who had pillaged and sacked much of the European coastline were settling down. By the Treaty of St-Clair-sur-Epte in AD 911, territory in northern France was granted to a marauding band of Vikings led by a chief named Rollo. The Vikings settled in an area that became known as Normandy. In the continual twist of history, the former destroyers became builders of churches, monasteries and castles. By 1066, one Norman duke was established and powerful enough to successfully invade England. There were several other factors:

- The spread of Christianity. Part of settling down in those times was to accept Christianity and, increasingly, European countries outside the old Roman Empire did just that. In AD 988 the Russian Prince Vladimir was baptised. Poland opted for Christianity in AD 966, and King Stephen of Hungary was converted in the year 1000, as was the Viking assembly of Iceland.

- Population pressure. Population in England rose from around 1.5 million in the year 1000 to around 4 million by the time of the Black Death in 1348. During the same period in Europe, it increased from around 30 million to around 73 million.

- Stone was available. Much of the stone used in early English construction came from Caen, but later English quarries were discovered, such as Stamford and Lincolnshire.

The eagle lectern.

Building Style

Just as the terms Stone, Bronze and Iron Age were first used in the early nineteenth century to aid the understanding of prehistory, at the same time names were given to various architectural styles to aid the understanding of building structures. Romanesque architecture (late tenth century to early twelfth) can be identified right across Europe by, amongst other things, round arches (as used by the Romans), thick walls and sturdy piers. In England it is known as Norman because it was introduced by the Norman conquerors. Southwell's nave (the western part of the church generally used by the greater part of the congregation) is an excellent example of this style, as is the north porch through which you will enter.

The Gothic style (twelfth to fifteenth century) was known at the time as the French style, and its characteristic features are pointed arches, flying buttresses (arched wall supports that enable larger and more ornate windows to be inserted in them) and ribbed vaults (more complicated ceiling patterns, in simple terms!). Southwell's Quire (between the nave and the High Altar at the eastern end of the church) was rebuilt in 1234 in Gothic style. The Chapter House (the monks' meeting room) has Gothic stone vaulting. So, like almost all English cathedrals, Southwell has a mixture of styles because it was built and adapted over a very long period of time. This contrasts to Italian, French and German cathedrals which were constructed in much shorter time periods (Salisbury is an English exception, completed in only thirty-eight years).

Eagle Lectern

Edward VI (1547-53) continued the country's shift towards Protestantism by attempting to eliminate all traces of idolatry. Almost all statues, icons, prayer books and other books and manuscripts were destroyed. Many ornate rood screens (separating the clergy at the altar from the congregation) were ripped out in an attempt to emphasise a closer relationship between the priests and their flock. Wall paintings were whitewashed over and valuable gold and silverware was sold off or melted down. The congregation of Southwell Minster would have worshipped in a church that seemed bare and quiet.

In 1750 the Eagle Lectern, which now stands proudly in the choir area of Southwell Cathedral, was rescued from the bottom of the lake in Newstead Abbey where it had been thrown by monks in the sixteenth century for protection!

Visiting

The minster is open every day, £3 voluntary contribution. Excellent visitor centre – refreshments and guidebook available. On the second Friday of the month, Southwell has a farmers' market.

SOUTHWELL WORKHOUSE

This is the best example of a surviving workhouse in Britain. Built in 1824, it now looks so clean and refreshing from the outside that it is, at first, hard to imagine the misery that many of the inmates had to endure. The inside is also clean but an audio tour takes the visitor back to the harsh realities of the nineteenth and early twentieth centuries. Southwell's workhouse poses the question that countries around the world had to grapple with – how should society deal with the poor and needy? This is a big subject which the Southwell Workhouse experience addresses in a building that saw some help and a lot of misery over 200 years.

'Please, sir, I want some more.'

Charles Dickens detected the inhumanity of the workhouse and wrote *Oliver Twist* in 1837 in order to expose what was happening. Nine-year-old Oliver and his fellow paupers were fed three meals of thin gruel a day, with an onion twice a week and half a bread roll on Sundays. It wasn't designed to build them up, but to keep them alive. The boys cast lots to decide who should complain and Oliver was chosen:

Southwell Workhouse.

The master aimed a blow at Oliver's head with the ladle; pinioned him in his arm; and shrieked aloud for the beadle. The board were sitting in solemn conclave, when Mr. Bumble rushed into the room in great excitement, and addressing the gentleman in the high chair, said, 'Mr. Limbkins, I beg your pardon, sir! Oliver Twist has asked for more!' There was a general start. Horror was depicted on every countenance. 'For more!' said Mr. Limbkins. 'Compose yourself, Bumble, and answer me distinctly. Do I understand that he asked for more, after he had eaten the supper allotted by the dietary?' 'He did, sir,' replied Bumble. 'That boy will be hung,' said the gentleman in the white waistcoat. 'I know that boy will be hung.'

Help?

For thousands of years the poor and needy would have sought help from their close and wider family. Later, one's fellow villagers, religious leaders, craft guilds and manorial lord could have helped in bad times.

In the sixteenth century, England was undergoing changes that would eventually lead to the Industrial Revolution, such as the conversion of arable land into pasture. Landlords enclosed their land in order to keep sheep and make improvements. The wool fetched a good price but it meant there was less need for agricultural workers. As many workers were now wage earners instead of being tied to an estate, they became unemployed. The second half of the sixteenth century also saw a steady rise in inflation. Because most manual workers were on fixed rates of pay, any rise in prices meant they were worse off. Towards the end of the century there were several periods of bad harvests, causing corn prices to rise steeply, adding to the terrible problems of the poor.

From 1536-39, Henry VIII destroyed many of the monasteries after he broke away from the Roman Catholic Church. It meant that part of the country's support system broke down just as the country was experiencing problems. There were complaints that the country was full of sturdy beggars, i.e. beggars who were able to work, not old or infirm. The Tudors grappled with this new problem. They tried branding and whipping beggars, enslaving them and putting them in the stocks for a few days. Houses of correction were set up (for example, Bridewell, London, in 1555) to remove beggars and idlers from the streets and punish them. This approach spread to Northern Europe and there was a constant fluctuation between help and punishment in both England and the continent over the next two centuries, with the accent being on the latter through workhouses and forced-labour schemes.

After a spell of poor harvests at the end of the sixteenth century, the government came reluctantly to the conclusion that destitution was a matter for the State to deal with, and Poor Law Acts were passed between 1597 and 1601. All parishioners were to be taxed so that each parish could maintain its own poor. Work was to be provided for the able-bodied and children were to be helped to find apprenticeships.

By 1784 Poor Law relief for England and Wales had grown to £2 million, by 1804 it was £4 million and by 1831 it was nearly £7 million. There were fears that it would become a burden on the country but the greater fear was that by providing relief, people could be motivated not to work – the basic assumption being that employment was available for all who sought it. This was indeed the view of the Royal Commission on which the 1834 Poor Law Act was based, as can be seen by the three core proposals:

- The situation of the pauper should be more unpleasant than the least well-off person in employment.

- The treatment of the poor should be standard throughout the country.

- No more relief to the able-bodied unless they entered a workhouse.

The 15,500 parishes were grouped into 643 unions so they could afford to build and run a workhouse on the above lines. The Victorian workhouse that Dickens satirised was born.

The tragic reality was that the ill, the old and infirm and children made up well over 80 per cent of the inmates and hence their lives were made miserable in order to deter the able-bodied from seeking help. Moreover, these ideas did not take into account unemployment caused by the massive changes that were taking place throughout the country. Nottinghamshire was the home of framework knitting, notoriously subject to periodic depression, and the country was in the throes of yet more land enclosures, causing even more job losses amongst the peasantry.

Visiting

A National Trust site with excellent facilities. For further information, visit www.nationaltrust. org.uk/workhouse or telephone (01636 817260).

STAPLEFORD CROSS

There is no visitor centre, no souvenir shop (but a good coffee bar in the health centre across the road), no car park and it doesn't even look like a cross; but, on the bright side, there are no admission charges and it is amongst the oldest medieval items in the county. As you stand and admire it consider that over a thousand years ago the locals may have travelled here to listen to a travelling preacher, possibly from Southwell. Yet for many years, perhaps hundreds, it lay neglected within the churchyard. A plaque in front of the cross tells its story.

Stone crosses are a great link to the pre-Norman days when the land was split between Christians and pagans. Even if Stapleford Cross is eleventh century, it may well have replaced an older monument, set up in the days before the Danes when Christianity was becoming established.

The Cross Symbol

A circle with a cross inside has been commonly used to represent the sun and the moon as a deity, the arms of the cross being the rays. The Egyptians used it to represent the rain god. The Celts used it as a symbol of the wheel, for them a sacred object. The cross became a common symbol of Christianity in the fourth century AD, but it was not adopted officially by the Church until AD 680. Some of the earliest Christian crosses were made using the first two letters of the word 'Christ', as per the Greek spelling – X (chi) and P (rho). These chi-rho crosses later developed to have the X in an upright position and the P being dropped. Finally the cross was encircled, helping with the manufacturing and carving process. A good example would be the Anglian cross at Sproxton, Leicestershire.

Timeline

- Fifth and sixth centuries – Saxons, Jutes and Angles invade Britain. They worshipped the Norse gods, Tiw (war), Thunor (thunder) and Woden (giver of victory).

- AD 563 – St Columba, a Celtic monk from Ireland, founded a new monastery on the island of Iona, from where a wave of conversions to Christianity began in northern Britain.

- AD 597 – Sent by the Pope, Augustine landed in Kent to begin the conversion of England from the south. Four years later, Paulinus arrived in England to help Augustine. He persuaded the King of Northumbria, Edwin, to allow him to settle in York and build a church there (Edwin's wife, Aethelberg, was a Christian).

- Seventh century AD – Northumbria flourished as a Christian community and a considerable number of stone crosses were erected and carved with great skill. An excellent example, the cross at Bewcastle with its undulating scrolls and carved figures, still stands, commemorating King Egfrith (AD 670-85). The Revd Hill, writing in 1905, compared Stapleford's cross to the Bewcastle one, seeing similarities in design (interlacing patterns). He also knew that Mercia began to adopt Christianity after the pagan King Penda had been killed in battle in AD 655. He reasoned that crosses would have been erected in Nottinghamshire at that time, and hence dated Stapleford's cross to between AD 680 and 780.

Sproxton Cross.

Dating Difficulties

Writing in 1945, J. Holland Walker came up with another theory. He argued that the Northumbrian crosses were special, were confined to that kingdom (apart from one exception) and that their production ceased after the pagan Danes overran much of the country in the ninth century. King Alfred (AD 871-99) stopped the Danish advance and his successors gradually extended the Anglo-Saxon kingdom. During the tenth century, the Danish area, the Danelaw, and the Saxon area merged into one kingdom. By the eleventh century Christianity was once again the norm. The Danes admired the Northumbrian crosses and began to produce a whole series of their own. These Anglo-Saxon/Danish crosses were not in the same class as the earlier Northumbrian crosses. He concluded that Stapleford's cross was of this later type, probably from Cnut's time (1016-35). During his reign, many previously destroyed churches were rebuilt and Christian rites restored.

How Many?

Alfred Rimmer, in his authoritative work on the subject written in 1875, was able to say that 'there were probably not fewer than five thousand crosses in England'. Because crosses were erected for so many reasons in the Middle Ages, there was at least one in every town or village and hence his guesstimate is likely to be true. He also laments that so many have been lost since the fourteenth century, some destroyed during the Dissolution of the Monasteries, many others meeting the same fate at the hands of the Puritan extremists in the mid-seventeenth century.

Colston Basset Cross.

Types of Crosses

- Market Crosses. They served to remind people to conduct their business fairly and were convenient places for town officials to collect market tolls. In medieval times, Nottinghamshire had thirty townships with market rights, but this had reduced to ten by 1790 – Nottingham, Newark, Southwell, Bingham, Blyth, Mansfield, Ollerton, East Retford, Tuxford and Worksop. A market cross still stands at Colston Basett. Much renovated, it is still partly medieval, and was the first site to be owned by the National Trust in Nottinghamshire.

- Commemorative crosses. A good example would be the Eleanor crosses. Eleanor was Edward I's Queen. Together they had fifteen children, of whom only six survived. She accompanied him on all his expeditions, even to the Holy Land. She died at Harby, Nottinghamshire, in 1290 on her way to meet her husband in Scotland. The King decided to erect a series of crosses on the route of her funeral procession to London. Of the twelve crosses, only three remain – the ornate, decorated crosses at Geddington, Hardingstone and Waltham.

- Preaching crosses. Before churches were erected, clergy would travel throughout their area preaching and attempting to make converts. Perhaps times and dates were pre-arranged. Stapleford's cross is almost certainly an example of this type.

Visiting

Many fragments or remnants of pre-Norman crosses or other artefacts exist today in the counties that once made up Mercia and Northumbria, but especially so in North Yorkshire, Cheshire, Cumbria, Derbyshire, Lincolnshire and Leicestershire. Breedon on the Hill in Leicestershire has several cross fragments and the largest known collection of Anglo-Saxon frieze and architectural carvings in the United Kingdom. In Nottinghamshire, parts of old stone crosses can be found in the churches of Bilsthorpe, East Bridgford, Hawksworth, Kneesal, North Leverton, Rolleston, Screveton and Shelford.

STOKE FIELD

There is no footpath or right of way over the battlefield, nor is it laid out with markers and information boards. At the nearby church, where many soldiers sharpened their swords before the battle, there is a simple headstone for the 7,000 dead, totally inadequate to commemorate such a huge loss of life. What was it all about? Why did over 5,000 foreigners come here to die for an English cause? The answers reveal some fascinating truths about England and Europe in the fifteenth century.

There is still something to see here. The line of high ground, covered by trees, upon which the rebels began the battle, is still prominent. At the end of the battle, many rebels attempted to escape over this rise and down the gulleys that led towards Fiskerton Crossing. So many were slaughtered by the pursuing King's army that one track was known as the Red Gutter. This site is important. You are walking on a site where around 14,000 men fought a ferocious battle in 1487 to decide whether or not an impostor would take over as King of England.

There are no facilities here. Fifty miles away on Bosworth Field, where Henry VII defeated King Richard III two years before, there are information boards, a visitor centre and a recreated medieval village. Unlike at Bosworth, the Battle of Stoke didn't unseat a King but, by seeing off a serious challenge to Henry's crown, it ended the Wars of the Roses, thereby embarking England upon a period of relative peace during which she took several steps towards becoming an important global power.

Timeline

- 1455 – Wars of the Roses begin. Two family dynasties with claims to the throne of England fought seventeen major battles over the following twenty-two years.

- 1422-61 – Henry VI, House of Lancaster.

- 1461-70 – Edward IV, House of York.

- 1470-71 – Henry VI, House of Lancaster.

- 1471-83 – Edward IV, House of York.

- 1483 – Edward V, House of York.

- 1483-85 – Richard III, House of York.

- 1485 – Henry VII wins the Battle of Bosworth and becomes King. He is a Lancastrian but his father is Edmund Tudor, so he becomes the first King in the Tudor dynasty.

- 1486 – Henry marries Elizabeth of York in an attempt to unite the two rival houses.

- 1487 – Battle of Stoke Field. A Lancastrian victory prevented the civil war dragging on.

The Battle

Two years after Henry VII had won the Battle of Bosworth he faced a very serious threat to his position from a baker's son. In one of the most audacious acts in English history, Lambert Simnel attempted to impersonate the Yorkist heir to the throne, the would-be Edward VI. (Edward was reported to have died in the Tower, but King Henry paraded him in London to prove otherwise!)

The pretender had the backing of Margaret, Duchess of Burgundy, a Yorkist living in France and hence able to plot against the throne in safety. With her enormous wealth, she hired 2,000 German mercenaries and, together with up to 4,000 Irish levies, they landed in Lancashire in June 1487 to join up with the Yorkist army. However, less than 2,000 English troops were waiting, far fewer than had been hoped for.

The Earl of Lincoln led his rebel army towards Newark to cross the Trent on the way to London. Realising the danger, Henry hurried to intercept. Passing Nottingham, he was joined by many of the shire's important landowners, including Gervase Clifton, Henry Willoughby

TO COMMEMORATE
THE DEAD AT STOKE FIELD
16TH JUNE 1487

JOHN DE LA POLE
EARL OF LINCOLN
SIR THOMAS GERALDINE
COL. MARTIN SCHWARTZ
AND 7000 OTHERS
ENGLISH IRISH AND GERMAN

Memorial
headstone.

and William Pierrepont, with their armed retainers. The King's army made camp at Radcliffe on Trent, where a minor panic ensued following a rumour that the rebels were about to attack.

Lincoln's army crossed the Trent near Fiskerton – the river being wider and shallower than today – camped near East Stoke and made ready. On the 16 June the vanguard of the King's army advanced to within arrow range and the commander, the Earl of Oxford, ordered his archers to begin firing. The poorly-armed Irish suffered many casualties, forcing Lincoln to abandon the high ground and attack. The Irish were easily repulsed but the German mercenaries, probably the most highly trained troops on the battlefield, inflicted heavy losses on the King's troops. The battle lasted about three hours and fighting must have been ferocious, because around 4,000 rebel soldiers were slain and up to 3,000 of Henry's army. Much of the slaughter took place at the end as the rebels fled down gullies in the escarpment towards the river. The German mercenaries, under Captain Shwartz, chose to stand and fight. Shwartz died and, it is thought, only about 200 mercenaries survived the day.

After the battle, Simnel was not executed, but made to work in the King's kitchen as a 'turn spit'.

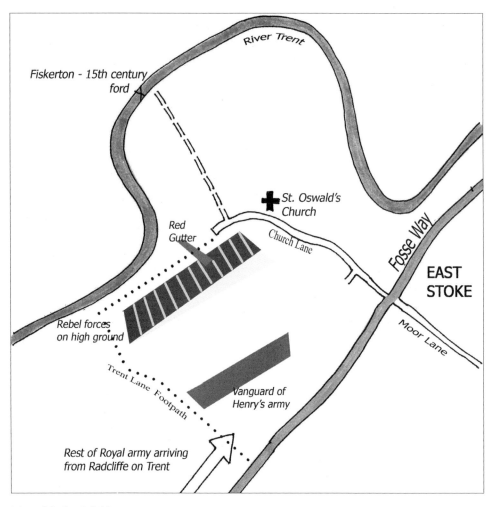

Map of the battlefield.

Who Did the Fighting?

The rebel army consisted of mercenaries, Irish levies and the private retinues of some Lancastrian noblemen. During the fifteenth century, the use of mercenaries in European warfare increased. Kings and rebels alike were tempted by the professionalism of these troops who came with their own weapons. The Swiss had a well-known, fearsome reputation, developed during the Hundred Years War. The Germans too had bands of soldiers available for hire. They fought in deep columns with 18ft pikes or two-handed axes, although by the end of the fifteenth century some would have had crossbows and early firearms.

Henry too had mercenaries, but also relied heavily on the private armies of his main supporters. Because many British dukes and barons had large retinues of servants who were actually their own private armies, they were able to live outside the law. People were afraid to challenge them, and hence disputes over the succession to the crown easily descended into warfare. When Henry VII came to the throne he passed laws against keeping too many retainers and established the Court of Star Chamber in which the King and the common people could challenge the authority of the nobles. He also appointed Justices of the Peace on a nationwide scale to see that the laws of the land were obeyed. By these means he ensured a period of stability in the realm, which enabled the economy to grow.

The Irish levies were the private armies of the Irish lords. By the end of the fifteenth century the area over which the English held sway was barely fifty miles square centred on Dublin, known as the Pale. Beyond the Pale, the Irish and Anglo-Irish lords battled one another. They came to dislike the remote rule by England and when an opportunity came to fight the English, the native Irish were only too eager.

A Second Imposter

Ten years after Lambert Simnel was captured at Stoke Fields, Perkin Warbeck attempted to impersonate Edward IV's son, Richard. Backed by 8,000 Yorkist suppporters, he landed in Devon in 1497, proclaiming himself King Richard IV. However, they lost their nerve when Henry VII approached with his well-trained troops. Warbeck was hanged in 1499.

Visiting

A footpath from Church Lane takes you behind the ridge, and you can return to the busy A46 via the Trent Lane track. OS Explorer Map 271 shows precise details.

THE PARK

If you were a member of Nottingham's well-to-do in the seventeenth and eighteenth centuries and dwelled in the town, then the place to live was on the periphery, such as Castle Gate and Low Pavement. The old-town area around St Mary's Church was ideal, with plenty of space for large mansions surrounded by fields (see Badder and Peat's 1744 map of the Lace Market). In the late eighteenth and early nineteenth centuries, various developments were to destroy this urban haven. The growth of the textile industry caused a great number of working people to cram into the overcrowded slums of the Rookeries, north of Parliament Street, and Narrow Marsh. This made the nearby old town area less desirable and the well-to-do began to look elsewhere. The textile manufacturers saw an opportunity. They used their growing wealth to buy up the landed houses in the old-town, and erect tall industrial buildings to make the best use of the space. The development of the Lace Market meant quality housing was needed elsewhere.

Ever since the Normans built their castle in the 1080s, the area to the west, now known as The Park, was the castle's private estate, where roaming deer could be hunted for the table. In 1809 the fourth Duke of Newcastle allowed the castle moat to be filled-in near the gatehouse so that a better access road into the grounds could be constructed. The Duke had plans to erect a select residential area. In 1825 he engaged architect Peter Robinson, who produced a plan and soon began to build a number of houses on the Ropewalk, Park Terrace and Park Valley. By 1832, around fifty houses had been built, but then building ceased. The year before, rioters from the town had set fire to the Duke's mansion in revenge for his voting against the Reform Bill. The house had been gutted and the Duke lost interest in his project.

To His Grace the Duke of Newcastle

This Print being the first of a series of four Views of NOTTINGHAM PARK, is most respectfully dedicated

By his obedient Servant

Thoˢ Forman

The Park estate in 1850, showing Park Valley, Lenton Road and the castle. (Courtesy of Picture the Past, NTGM009727)

In the 1840s there was much talk about the impending Enclosure Bill, without which the communal fields surrounding the town could not be developed. The Bill, passed in 1845 but not implemented until 1865 because of various disputes, led to land, previously worked communally, becoming available for sale and development. Prior to the Act, there were worries that, with increased supply, the price of land could fall. The Duke needed to develop The Park quickly. In 1854 he appointed T.C. Hine, an architect with a growing reputation, to be the estate's surveyor. His plans took into account the topological features of the site, and the number of houses began to increase again. It became one of the most sought-after places to live for the newly rich. During the 1880-95 boom years, mansions were erected for Frank Bowden, Jesse Boot and John Player. By the time Hine retired in 1891, there were few plots left for sale.

T.C. Hine

The nineteenth century was a period when the British economy underwent rapid expansion, especially so in the industrial Midlands and the North. Fortunes were made, towns prospered and this was reflected in the buildings. Not just the private dwellings, but also Town Halls, industrial buildings, pumping stations and railway stations. This was a time to show off your success. Architects were given a challenge and throughout the country they produced some excellent work; for example, Watt's warehouse in Manchester, with each storey in a different style (Italian Renaissance, Elizabethan, French Renaissance and Flemish) and each corner topped by a large tower, and St Pancras Railway Station, built with pride, reflecting a society brimming with confidence.

Nottingham's premier architect for the period was Hine. The superb Adams and Page warehouse on Stoney Street (now a college), the warehouses on the street of Broadway, Nottingham Corn Exchange, the restyled front of the Shire Hall, the restyled interior of the castle, Great Northern Station on London Road (now a nightclub) and All Saints Church, Raleigh Street, are just some of his surviving buildings that demonstrate his impact. Ken Brand's short booklet lists many more, but The Park estate is the best place to see his style. Around 200 houses in The Park are designed by him, some individually and others in a crescent or row, built to a pattern. Others in the estate were influenced by his style as he approved the designs.

New Homes for All

When the Enclosure Bill was finally passed, it was the wealthy section of society which most benefited. The three big estates of Alexandra Park (Mapperly), Mapperley Park and The Park were aimed at the rich middle classes. However, changes eventually benefited the poor too. In the Borough's plan there was provision for public parks (Arboretum and the Forest Recreation Ground) and a continuous tree-lined walk joining St Anne's with the Arboretum via Robin Hood's Chase, Corporation Oaks and Elm Avenue (it is still there). Next came the Forest district. In the early twentieth century the houses on the site bounded in the south by Gregory Boulevard were erected, intended for professional people such as teachers. The second phase (1905-14), bounded by Noel Street and Sherwood Rise, was aimed at the skilled and semi-skilled. These people were also catered for by the expansion of housing in the peripheral villages such as Basford, Radford, Lenton, etc. Eventually these grew to such an extent that they became suburbs of Nottingham, and the 1877 Borough Extension Act confirmed this. Nottingham's extended area now covered 10,935 acres (was 1,996 acres) and its population rose from 86,620 to 157,000.

The Park – Other Features

Let us get back to The Park. As well as houses by Hine, it also features designs by another famous Nottingham architect, Watson Fothergill. In all it has sixty-two listed buildings and in 1969 was designated a Conservation Area (later deemed to be of outstanding importance in the national context).

It also has the largest gas street-lighting system in Europe, being one of only two gas-lit areas in the country. Gas lighting was first installed in a factory in 1803 and spread to illuminate most towns in the nineteenth century. Electric lighting was invented in the 1870s but it took a long time for towns to incur the expense of the changeover. Nottingham switched to electric lights in 1937 but The Park, being private, elected to stay with gas, and now has a truly nineteenth-century ambience in the evening.

The Park also has a series of caves known as Lenton Hermitage, possibly inhabited by monks from Lenton Priory in the thirteenth century. Built into the rock on Castle Boulevard, they are tucked away from view behind various retail units.

Please respect this as a private residential estate and do not park your car within it – you will be fined. To identify the houses designed by Hine or Fothergill, consult *The Park Estate* by Ken Brand (page 29 and map).

TRENT BRIDGE CRICKET GROUND

International sport on a global scale began in the nineteenth century, and today over 200 countries compete in the Olympic Games. Cricket was one of the first global sports and the story of its development helps us understand the importance of Trent Bridge. This world-famous ground is one of the earliest established venues of any sport still hosting international games.

William Clark started it all by marrying the landlady of the Trent Bridge Inn, thereby obtaining the piece of land behind it. Officially opened in 1841, matches began on the ground in 1838, enabling Nottinghamshire to enter the County Championships. There were only two other counties involved – Sussex and Kent. By the mid-1860s there were eight first-class cricket counties and a continuous record of County Champions. In 1873 the MCC (English governing body) attempted to start a knockout cup competition, perhaps influenced by the success of the Football Association's cup. It didn't work out and finally, in 1895, the MCC recognised the championship, which involved fourteen counties. There are now eighteen.

Since 1890 Nottinghamshire have been County Champions five times, but their glory years were between 1865 and 1889 when they were champions fifteen times. All these achievements were made at Trent Bridge – the ground that hosted its first international cricket match (between England and Australia) in 1895. It was also the venue for the first game of the first-ever five match Test series between the same two countries, making it the third oldest ground to be used as a Test venue after Lords and Eden Gardens in Calcutta. W.G. Grace, acknowledged as the greatest player in the world during his era, played in that game at the age of fifty years and 320 days – his last ever Test. It has hosted more than 1,400 first class games, and still retains an aura of a bygone era. Despite recent improvements you can still experience the most traditional of English sports in one of the most traditional venues of any sport in the world.

The Game's Early Days

The game grew up on the estates of the great landowners in south-east England during the seventeenth century. From friendly matches between village teams the game spread to the universities, where organised sport was seen as character-building. Graduates spread the game throughout the country and by 1850 there were twenty-one clubs.

As early as the 1730s, the Artillery Ground in London was enclosed so spectators could be charged admission. With money involved, professional players emerged. To secure their services, some good players were given jobs on the team owners' estates, such as groom or bailiff. To increase the number of paying spectators, it became the fashion in the eighteenth century to name a team after the county in which it was based. So a match between two village teams could be labelled, for example, Hampshire vs. Surrey. In 1744, on the Artillery Ground, this process of talking-up a game was taken a stage further. The 'greatest cricket match ever known',

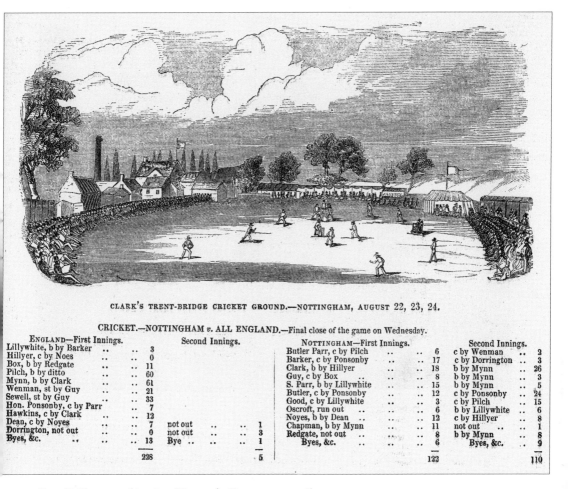

CLARK'S TRENT-BRIDGE CRICKET GROUND.—NOTTINGHAM, AUGUST 22, 23, 24.

CRICKET.—NOTTINGHAM v. ALL ENGLAND.—Final close of the game on Wednesday.

ENGLAND—First Innings.		Second Innings.		NOTTINGHAM—First Innings.		Second Innings.	
Lillywhite, b by Barker	3			Butler Parr, c by Pilch	6	c by Wenman	2
Hillyer, c by Noes	0			Barker, c by Ponsonby	17	c by Dorrington	3
Box, b by Redgate	11			Clark, b by Hillyer	18	b by Mynn	26
Pilch, b by ditto	60			Guy, c by Box	8	b by Mynn	3
Mynn, b by Clark	61			S. Parr, b by Lillywhite	15	b by Mynn	5
Wenman, st by Guy	21			Butler, c by Ponsonby	12	c by Ponsonby	24
Sewell, st by Guy	33			Good, c by Lillywhite	3	c by Pilch	15
Hon. Ponsonby, c by Parr	7			Oscroft, run out	6	b by Lillywhite	6
Hawkins, c by Clark	12			Noyes, b by Dean	12	c by Hillyer	8
Dean, c by Noyes	7	not out	1	Chapman, b by Mynn	11	not out	1
Dorrington, not out	0	not out	3	Redgate, not out	8	b by Mynn	8
Byes, &c.	13	Bye	1	Byes, &c.	6	Byes, &c.	9
	228		5		122		110

Trent Bridge ground in 1842. (Picture the Past, NTGM010238)

according to the press, was played between a team raised by the Sackville family of Sevenoaks, labelled as Kent, and the Rest of England. Kent were the winners by one wicket. Teams labelled Kent, Surrey, Sussex and Hampshire continued to play against 'The Rest' until the second decade of the nineteenth century. Then, in 1825, a match was arranged between Sussex and Kent, since hailed as the beginning of the County Championship. In the 1830s, the team from Nottingham was building up a reputation by beating all the other Midland teams. It challenged Sussex and became the third team in the championship.

Cricket Conquers the World?

The first international match took place in 1844 between USA and Canada in New Jersey. Introduced to North America by English colonists in the sevententh century, there were enough players to provide opposition to the first ever English touring side in 1859. However, disruption caused by the American Civil War (1861–65) enabled baseball to gain popularity rather than cricket.

Trent Bridge Pavilion, built 1873.

Elsewhere in the British Empire, the game reached India in the eighteenth century via employees of the British East India Company, Australia after 1788 and New Zealand and South Africa in the early nineteenth century. The Netherlands established a cricket league in 1883 and, among others, Denmark, Papua New Guinea and Kenya also developed the game.

Stadiums

The capacity of Trent Bridge has just increased from 15,000 to 17,500. This is less than Old Trafford (22,000) and The Oval (23,000) but compares favourably with Headingley (17,000). England's highest capacity Test ground is Lords (32,000). These figures are lower than comparable football grounds, but then spectators do spend the whole day at a cricket match, not just a couple of hours. However, other countries have stadiums with greater capacities – AMI Stadium, Christchurch, New Zealand (36,000), Eden Park, Auckland (48,000), Sydney Cricket Ground (46,000), and Melbourne Cricket Ground (100,000). Eden Gardens, Calcutta, used to have a capacity of 120,000, reflecting the huge popularity of the game there, but, following improvements, the revised capacity is 90,000. The largest capacity stadium for any sport (outside racing circuits) is in Pyongyang, North Korea (150,000), followed by Calcutta's Salt Lake Stadium (120,000), which plays host to football and athletics. Interestingly, five of the next six highest capacity stadiums are in the United Sates and play host to American football.

A set of rules existed in 1744 detailing the length of the pitch, the size of the wicket, the number of balls per over and weight of the ball. Thereafter, certain rules were changed to cope with circumstances. For example, in September 1771 Thomas White of Reigate arrived at the crease with a bat that was the same width as the wicket. Immediately a law was passed to limit the bat size to 4½in. Three years later, when players were deliberately obstructing the wicket with their legs, it was decreed that a batsman could be 'out' leg-before-wicket.

Prior to 1760, bowling was by under-arm delivery along the ground, which is why early bats looked like hockey sticks. After 1760, players could vary the line, the length and the pace of the delivery. In the 1820s it became the fashion to bowl with the arm coming round the body and this was made legal in 1835. Over-arm bowling was adopted in 1864.

Viewing

Tours are held every Tuesday afternoon, costing £2. Book in advance at the shop or telephone (0115 9819939). Also see a game at Trent Bridge or one of the 100 or so cricket grounds in the county (in the 1950s, there were 366 grounds). Be careful, if you like statistics you could get hooked. For the Box Office, telephone (0115 9823000).

THE TRIP TO JERUSALEM

Which is the oldest inn in England still serving ale? Many people would immediately mention the Trip to Jerusalem. The most certain thing you can say about the Trip is that it is famous. The name itself conjures up thoughts of crusaders meeting up for a final drink before heading off for the Holy Land. It even states clearly on the side of the extremely photogenic building, 'The Oldest Inn in England – 1189'. Could a place continually advertise this if there were no truth in it? True or not, photos of the sign and peoples' stories of their visits have spread far and wide. Before I made my first trip to the town in the 1960s, I was told by my barber in Sussex to be sure to visit the Trip.

Early Brewing

Beer goes back a long way. Apparently studies of residues found at prehistoric sites in the Far East have dated beer to 5000 BC. The Sumerians and the Egyptians brewed beer before it spread to Europe. Recent research has revealed over 4,000 microbreweries in Ireland serving local communities around 1500 BC. Certainly brewing was a localised affair in the Middle Ages, as was flour grinding and bread making. But whereas these trades were restricted to certain premises only, the brewing of ale was less restricted. If someone had the facilities, they could brew a batch of ale, hang a sign outside and become an alehouse for a period. Inns, by contrast, were generally purpose-built with extra bedrooms to accommodate travellers and some stabling. Some of the earliest monasteries would have served as inns, their brewhouses supplying their guesthouses. From around the fourteenth century, some inns and alehouses would have displayed a pictorial sign by which they could be identified. The 1552 Alehouse Act required an outlet to have a licence from the local justices in order to be able to sell to the public. The term 'public house' was soon shortened to 'pub'. So, if we are looking for an ancient pub, we need an ancient building known to have been associated with brewing, possibly a monastery or a castle.

The Trip to Jerusalem.

How Do Nottingham's Pubs Shape Up?

- The Trip. There were once three pubs in the area known as the Brewhouse Yard. One, the Pilgrim, appeared on Deering's plan of Nottingham in 1751. According to historian J.H. Walker, writing in 1928:

  > Brewhouse Yard itself was an extraordinary little area… legally outside the jurisdiction of the town… used by the 'Philadelphians' whose particular shibboleth (by which they hoped to reach heaven) was to refer to each other as Brother Pilgrim. By a series of curious legal chances, Brewhouse Yard came under jurisdiction of a court held in Cotgrave (which was under the headship of the Prior of Jerusalem) – and I think that some nickname concocted from 'The Pilgrim' and this Order of Jerusalem is the origin of the present name of the inn.

  When the pub was sold again in 1834, the present name was on the deeds of sale. By 1909 there were only two pubs in the area, the Trip and the Hanging Gate, both ancient rock houses with brick and timber fronts dating back 250 years or so. The Trip is the sole survivor today.

What can we suppose is likely? The building is in the right position at the foot of the rock (an area still called the Brewhouse Yard today) where brewing and malting were very likely carried out to serve the castle retainers. From an early age the castle's caves would have been ideal both for brewing ale and storing it. The chances are that some of the ale was sold to the locals from premises on this site. The castle was rebuilt in stone during the twelfth century, so a working brewhouse at that time is a definite possibility.

- The Bell. Behind the Regency façade (1810-20) is a building that was once the refectory of the Carmelite Friary founded in 1272 on Beastmarket Hill. The caves are the oldest part of the building, stretching back the whole length of the inn. They contain two wells from which natural spring waters were once obtained for on-site brewing. After the Dissolution of the Monasteries in 1536, the premises became a secular alehouse, known as the Angel (from Latin *angelus*, meaning noonday bell. The bell tolled at set hours to call the friars to prayer). The pub's main building has been dated to the early 1400s, but it is thought that the flagstones in the entrance passageway are the originals. The first mention of the current name was in 1638. In summary, this is another venue that could well have been selling beer to the public at an early age, possibly the thirteenth century – slightly later than the possible date for the Trip!

- Ye Old Salutation. The date displayed on the wall is 1240, but this is the date of the first building on the site, the home of a master tanner. The oldest timber of the current building has been dated to 1360, when it is not thought to have been an alehouse, nor was it referred to as such in the Borough record of 1414. Some time before 1649 ale was sold here, because on that date the innkeeper changed the name from the Salutation to the Soldier and Citizen. Beneath the building is a cave which may well have been used to brew ale and store it.

- Newark's White Hart has a roof dated to 1350, but the old part is no longer a pub. The building of Newark's Woolpack Inn dates to around 1450, but began life as a rich merchant's house. The Angel Inn, Blyth, was the site of twelfth/thirteenth century inn but the present building is only about 250 years old.

Around the country a new book, *Licensed to Sell,* by Brandwood, Davison and Slaughter, examines the rival claims of six pubs to be the oldest pub in Britain – Ye Olde Fighting Cocks, St Albans; the Old Ferry Boat, Holywell, Cambridge; the Eagle and Child, Stow-on-the-Wold; the Bingley Arms, Bardsey, Leeds; the Skirrid Mountain Inn, Llanfihangel Crocorney, near Abergavenny; and Ye Olde Trip to Jerusalem.

Visiting
As no one can give a definite answer as to which pub in the land is the oldest, the safest thing to do is visit them all. The things we have to do for history! For the purposes of this county a good itinerary is to visit the three Nottingham city venues. The Trip, being built into the rock, requires no specific tour. The Salutation will open up its caves on request, telephone in advance (0115 9881948). To arrange a tour of the medieval cellars in the Bell, telephone ahead (0115 9475241).

WOLLATON HALL

In 1487 Henry VII won the Battle of Stoke Field, signalling the end of the Wars of the Roses and taking England into a period of political stability, during which she evolved from a state on the sidelines of European history to one that would dominate much of the world in the coming centuries. The superb Elizabethan building that is Wollaton Hall is a monument to this new era. In previous centuries, manor houses were built with moats and towers so the local magnate had a base from which his military retainers could defend his territory. However, Wollaton Hall was not built with defence in mind, but to impress, a sign that the unsettled lawlessness of the Middle Ages was coming to an end. It is also a showcase of a new building style, one that encompassed much of Europe. In addition it plays host to two other attractions – Nottingham's Natural History Museum and Industrial Museum – and even has a link to the age of discovery. Recently superbly renovated, this is a place to return to time and again.

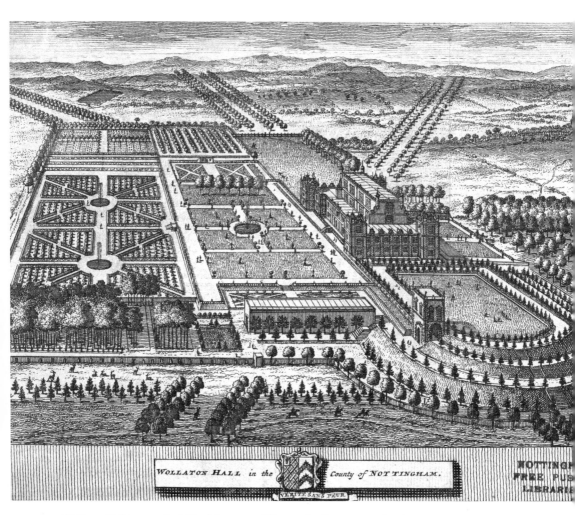

Wollaton Hall in 1707 by J. Kip. (Courtesy of Picture the Past, NTGM008717)

The Willoughbys

One of the families who benefited from the new political stability were the Willoughbys, an ancient Nottinghamshire family. Following the Battle of Stoke Field, Henry Willoughby was knighted and prospered to such a degree that he was able to entertain lavishly and travel to Rome. His wealth was increasingly based on the substantial revenues from coal produced in the Wollaton coalfields. In 1559 Henry's grandson, Francis, inherited the estate and, being only thirteen, was placed under the wardship of Sir Francis Knowele. Knowele was part of the Royal court of Queen Elizabeth, and young Francis, a newly-wealthy and highly-marriageable young man, experienced life in the court circle. After taking control of his estates he built up his fortune and acquired influence serving as a Justice of the Peace and also High Sheriff of Nottinghamshire. Obsessed with wealth and status, he wanted a new house to allow him to entertain and bestow favours on his followers.

Building Revolution

The sixteenth century saw a revolution in the building of houses for the very rich through much of Europe. The new demand was for style rather than defence. The change began in Italy, where new country houses were erected in the style of ancient Rome. This 'classical style' was soon regarded as the appropriate one for major buildings. The Italian architects compiled pattern books to demonstrate the styles to potential builders and these were circulated amongst the landowners of Europe.

Francis Willoughby wanted to show he was abreast of the latest architectural fashions, but, at the same time, he wanted traditional English features such as traceried windows, turrets, a Great Hall and a Great Chamber. To do this he needed someone capable of combining these different stylistic traditions. He found the perfect person in Robert Smythson.

Smythson had been involved in the building of Longleat and Bolsover Castle and later worked on Hardwick Hall. Wollaton was his first independent commission. He is buried in St Leonard's Church, Wollaton.

Court's Progress

In the sixteenth century, Queen Elizabeth's court still travelled around the country, 'on progress' as it was called, for eight to twelve weeks of the year, as did other European courts at that time. Court officials would draw up a list of the lucky ones to benefit from the prestige and expense of her visit. She would generally be accompanied by her servants, members of the Privy Council, up to 400 carts and around 300 packhorses and mules carrying everything from the Queen's wardrobe to her legal documents and bath. Willoughby hoped Wollaton Hall would be chosen.

It was, but not until 1603. Queen Anne called in on her way south from Scotland to join her husband, King James I, in London. Unfortunately for Francis, by then, both he and the Queen he designed the house for were dead.

Wollaton Manor and Wollaton Hall

The old manor house was a collection of buildings, mostly of wood and plaster, with leaded windows, busy with people and animals living side by side, and where people of all classes and occupations met. The new hall was designed to meet the new rules of etiquette which called for a stricter separation of the upper classes from the rest. But as well as greater privacy for the ruling family, the hall had to be capable of staging lavish entertainment. It achieved these aims through its design. The basement housed the kitchens and offices, the ground floor showed off the Great Hall for public ceremony and entertainment, leaving the upper floors for either public or private entertaining.

Whereas the old manor house was in close proximity to the bustling village of Old Wollaton, the new hall was at the top of a low hill surrounded by a formal garden within a vast area of parkland. It was one of the first Elizabethan grand houses to be built without a central courtyard. This allowed it to have a wonderful central tower, the Prospect Room, from which to view the surrounding symmetrical garden.

Over the course of history, Wollaton Hall was refurbished and redecorated to suit the needs of its various occupants. In 1641 a fire caused much destruction and it was abandoned for forty-four years. Cassandra Willoughby renovated it in 1687 during a period of greater prosperity. The brick stable block and estate offices were added in 1779 and the iron and glass Camellia House in 1823. Finally, in 1924, it was sold to the City of Nottingham and became the Museum of Natural History.

Connection to the Age of Discovery

In 1453 the Turks took control of Constantinople, blocking the spice route to the west and sending the prices of spices in Europe rocketing. If anyone could find an alternative route to the Spice Islands, they would make a fortune. The Portuguese succeeded when Vasco Da Gama rounded South Africa, and sailed on to India in 1499. Fifty years later, three English ships left London in May 1553, with Richard Chancellor and Hugh Willoughby (Henry Willoughby's half-brother) in command. Their aim was to find a north-east passage, over the top of Russia, into the Pacific. Willoughby and his crew froze to death in the attempt, but Chancellor returned to England in 1554 with letters from the Russian Czar promising trading privileges.

Other Elizabethan Examples

- Longleat. Elizabeth I honoured the house with a visit in 1574.

- Hardwick, Derbyshire, built between 1591 and 1597.

- Kirby Hall, Northamptonshire, one of England's greatest Elizabethan houses, again built to receive the Queen.

Visiting

The hall is open every day. Free entry, £2 for car park. There is a charge for some tours. All facilities are in the museum.

WORKSOP PRIORY CHURCH

In the fourteenth century the first sight of the priory for travellers emerging from Sherwood Forest would have been the gatehouse. And welcome it would have been too, for the forest had a reputation for robbers and thieves. Perhaps they took lodgings there for the night before visiting the magnificent, 360ft-long priory church. The church replaced a previous village

The splendid Norman arches of Worksop Priory.

church and was used daily by the monks, but it remained the church for the villagers. It was this that saved it from being completely destroyed in 1539 along with most of the other monastic buildings on this site (dormitory, refectory, bakehouse, library, etc.) and around the county. The current church is now much smaller, 135ft in length, but retains much of its Norman structure. The twin towers are still there bestriding a lovely Norman entrance, and the magnificent nave with its splendid Norman arches. The early fourteenth-century gatehouse has also survived, complete with little niches containing statues of St Augustine, St Cuthbert and others. The iconoclasts, looking to destroy such images, thankfully missed these.

The priory was founded between 1123 and 1140 by William de Lovetot near the village of Worksop, and was well-endowed with income and rents from various villages in the local area and in Normandy. One of twelve such monasteries established in the county, and one of hundreds established countrywide at this time, this excellent Norman building is the best link to that time.

Origins and Terms
Abbeys, priories and friaries are all monasteries. The abbey was largest in size or status, with a priory slightly smaller. The origins of monasticism are to be found in India, where Hinduism is thought to have evolved about 3000 BC. Buddhism started there in the sixth century BC. Its founder, Gautama Buddha, was born into a royal family but left his protected life to live as a homeless, holy man for many years, during which time he mixed with some of India's wandering Hindu ascetics.

These religious followers (or monks as they came to be called in the West, derived from Greek *monakhos*, meaning solitary) were attempting to adopt a simple, austere lifestyle in order to please their god. They indulged in practices more rigorous than religion demands for its normal followers, such as denying themselves too much food, the right to marry and the right to own property. However, after the death of Buddha, monks began to live together, initially in the rainy season, but later in permanent monasteries under an agreed set of rules. These became centres of knowledge and literacy, and gradually Buddhism and monasticism spread to China, Tibet, Japan and the West.

Timeline for Christian Monasticism

- AD 313 – Edict of Milan granted tolerance to Christians throughout the Roman Empire.

- AD 320 – Pachomius, an ex-Roman soldier, established one of the first communities of Christian monks at Tabennisi in Egypt. It would have been fairly small, with several single rooms or cells for the monks and enclosed by a wall. Simple monasteries then spread across the empire, which in the fourth century AD covered much of Europe, including Wales and Ireland.

- Sixth century AD – monasteries came to the British mainland, Iona (AD 563) and Canterbury (AD 597).

- Seventh and eighth centuries AD – monasteries spread throughout the land, acting as missionary bases and some as cathedrals. They became centres of learning and wealth.

- Ninth century AD – Vikings raided the British Isles. Monasteries were looted and destroyed, and monasticism collapsed.

- 1066-1200 – The golden age for the founding of monasteries in England. Numbers rose from around fifty to 500-600 as the Norman barons sought to show off their wealth and provide a place where people could pray for them in the afterlife. The Nottinghamshire monasteries were all founded in this period:

    1086-88 – Blyth Benedictine Priory
    1109-14 – Lenton Cluniac Priory
    1119-39 – Thurgaton Augustinian Priory
    1123-40 – Worksop Augustinian Priory
    1120-40 – Broadholme Premonstratensian
    1146 – Rufford Cistercian Abbey
    1150 – Wallingswell Benedictine Nunnery
    1156 – Felley Augustinian Priory
    1154-60 – Welbeck Premonstratensian Abbey
    1170 – Newstead Augustinian Priory
    1170 – Shelford Augustinian Priory
    1185-92 – Mattersey Gilbertine Priory

Mattersey Priory.

The Monastery Cycle of Reform

As so often happens when something new is established, the start-up is accompanied by lofty ideals and enthusiasm. The monks would work hard within a rigid system of prayer, manual work, learning and copying. However, as monasteries were left money by rich landowners in return for prayers said at their graves, their wealth accumulated, and monks' lifestyles became less strict. Some church people would react to this and attempt a reform.

In AD 529 St Benedict of Nursia set up a monastery in Monte Cassino in Italy. His rules, including poverty, chastity, obedience, stability and refraining from owning property, served as a model for most early, Western Christian monasteries. The Benedictines are still an important order today.

In 950 a new monastery was set up in Cluny, Burgundy, with the aim of getting back to the strict rules of the Benedictine Order. The Cluniacs grew in number and influence in Europe, even advising kings on reforms. Over time, however, this order too became wealthy and engaged in pomp and ceremony.

Another new broom appeared in the twelfth century, wielded by the Augustinians. Unlike most Benedictine and Cluniac monks, they preached in the communities and the local landowners used them as priests in their local church. They taught love and respect and the pursuit of truth through learning. Their name derived from St Augustin, who set up his first monastery in AD 388.

The Cistercians (founded in Citeaux in 1098) were another order attempting to get back to the basic Benedictine rules. They also showed an ascetic streak by banning warm underclothes under their white gowns. The order was very successful – by the late twelfth century there were over 500 houses throughout Europe, and one of their monks became Pope Eugene III in 1145.

Two other twelfth-century orders were modelled on the Cistercians. The Gilbertines, founded by St Gilbert, the parish priest of Sempringham, was the only purely English order. Thirteen houses of this order were set up during Gilbert's lifetime. The Premonstratensians (from Prémontré, France) chose remote sites and encouraged their monks to work on the land.

Worksop Priory had a well-known library, and one of its books still exists – the Tickhill Psalter, produced by John de Tickhill, Prior in the early 1300s. One of the finest of all English medieval manuscripts, richly decorated with colourful capitals and scenes from the life of King David, it is now kept in the New York Public Library.

Visiting

Please respect this working church. Check the Parish Office (01909 472180) to find out if there are any special services on. It is normally open Monday and Wednesday mornings and Saturday 9 a.m.–12 p.m.

MORE SITES

There are many other sites in the county which serve to illustrate the fascinating story of British history – Nottingham's medieval Severn Building, Colston Bassett's ruined church, Mansfield's The Maltings (the last purpose-built maltings to survive in the area) and many more. All have a story to tell beyond the actual building. Unfortunately, space does not permit me to list them all or develop their themes. However, below are a few of the ones that got away with a hint of the tales they have to tell.

Notts County Football Club

The first documented football club was in Edinburgh (1824). It no longer exists. In 1857 Sheffield FC formed. Both the English FA and FIFA officially recognise this club as the 'oldest now playing Association football' (in the Northern Counties East League). In 1862 Nottingham FC (later Nott's County FC) was founded. Along with the other clubs of the time they played a series of friendly matches. In 1885 it became legal to pay players and charge an entrance fee, so clubs opted to play against teams who could afford to pay them the most money, even if this meant calling off other, less lucrative, fixtures. In order to make sure that clubs fulfilled their fixtures, the Football League was formed in that same year. The founder members were Bolton Wanderers, Everton, Burnley, Accrington, Blackburn Rovers, Aston Villa, West Bromwich Albion, Wolverhampton Wanderers, Derby County, Stoke and Notts County. Of these, Notts County was the first club to be formed and this is the basis of their claim to be 'the oldest Football League club in the world'.

Notts County didn't move to their present ground, Meadow Lane, until 1910. Extensively renovated in 1994, its compactness evokes memories of the mid-twentiethth century when teams in all four divisions had big crowds (in the 1948/49 season, Notts County's average attendance was 29,976 while they were in Division 3). There are now 37,500 football clubs in England alone and countless others in the 208 member countries of FIFA. There are even 146 clubs on the tiny island of Tahiti!

This site leads into the fascinating story of football's development in English public schools and its spread throughout the country and the world. The ground is authentic, and while the stadium isn't, it is worth a trip to sample the atmosphere. If County win, you could be in for a real treat. Telephone the Box Office for ticket information (0115 9529000).

Opening of Meadow Lane Ground, 1910. (Picture the Past, NTGM011015)

Holme Pierrepont Hall.

Holme Pierrepont Hall

Built over 500 years ago, this is the oldest brick building in the county. Brick buildings began to be built in the twelfth and thirteenth centuries in Northern Europe, especially around the Baltic where there was a lack of local stone. Many brick-built churches and cathedrals have survived from this era in Sweden, Poland, Denmark, Russia and Germany. Brick building was also popular in the Low Countries, and ships exporting English wool to the continent would sometimes return with a cargo of bricks. Bricks being heavy, and medieval roads being very poor, transportation costs were expensive. Consequently, bricks were originally a luxury item, and during the fifteenth century they became quite fashionable as a building material in England. Herstmonceux Castle (1441) and Hampton Court Palace (begun in 1514) were among the first major brick buildings in England.

The art of brick-making spread to England via Dutch immigrants. As timber became scarce in Britain, bricks were increasingly used and became cheaper. It is thought that the bricks used for the construction of Holme Pierrepont Hall were locally produced. After the Great Fire of London in 1666 much of London was rebuilt with brick, but it was the Victorian period (1837–1901) that saw brick-built factories, warehouses and railway bridges become commonplace.

Another feature of the original Pierrepont Hall is the large number of tall chimneys, reflecting the widespread use of coal as fuel in the Tudor period. The chimneys were often clustered in groups and made into a feature. Today there are still many chimneys, but they no longer dominate.

There is so much more to this story. To visit you need to wait for the special open days held during the year, contact for details (0115 9332371). Leaflet available.

Carlton-in-Lindrick Church

A charming village name comprising four Saxon elements – 'ceorl' (free peasant), 'ton' (homestead), 'lin' (pool or lake) and 'rick' (narrow strip of land). Literally, it means 'a ceorl's homeland by a pool'. The church is lovely and in a beautiful setting, and was once thought to be a Saxon church. These are rare. The few which remain reasonably intact in the country include those at Bradford-on-Avon (Wiltshire), Barton-on-Humber (Humberside), Earl's Barton (Northamptonshire) and Bradwell-on-Sea (Essex).

And the others? From the Domesday Book we know that there were at least seventy-two churches in Nottinghamshire when William the Conqueror did his survey. Where were they? 'We can only infer that where our country church now stands, there in Saxon times often stood the timbered church of a Saxon thegn' (R.H. Hodgkin, *History of the Anglo-Saxons*). The timber churches would have been burnt down and the stone ones knocked down during the Viking raids.

Carlton-in-
Lindrick Church
tower.

Unitarian Church, Mansfield.

In 1954, historians D. Hamer and F. Scott took a closer look. They first focused on the tower's herring-bone masonry, a style where bricks or stone are placed in a zigzag fashion, and concluded that it could be either Norman or Saxon, but most probably Saxo-Norman – made by Saxon craftsmen under direct Norman supervision. They also thought that the tower's two small windows, crowned by semi-circular arches, were probably either Saxon windows from an earlier church inserted into the Norman fabric, or new, Norman windows, made to copy the Saxon style. Two of Lincoln's churches, St Mary Le Wigford and St Peter ad Gowts, were built after the conquest in the Saxon style.

So, we still have a Saxon/Norman church, probably built on the site of a previous Saxon church. The nave (the large western section), the chancel, the font and the splendid west doorway are all early Norman. The chancel of the church is unusually large. The Domesday Book lists six thegns with homes based in the village, so the church had to have enough clergy to serve these minor Anglo-Saxon noblemen. Yet thegns in Norman England were fast becoming rare as so many had been massacred on the 1066 battlefields. When William took over the country, the thegns were replaced by men loyal to him. Some emigrated, but most would have found themselves lower down the pecking order as sub-tenants, and subservient. The term thegn eventually died out. Again there is much more to this story.

Check with Southwell Diocesan Office (01636 814331) for a good time to visit. An information leaflet is available for a donation.

The Old Meeting House, Mansfield

Follow Stockwell Gate from the Market Place and, just past Westgate department store, slip between two buildings to enter Mill Walk. You will find a tree framing a lovely seventeenth-century building complete with the nameplate 'Old Meeting House' (Nonconformist places of worship were commonly called Meeting Houses, as so many services were held in private houses until the Toleration Act of 1689). This is not what you have come to see. This is the 'Old Parsonage,' once the home of Robert Porter, where Nonconformists met from the 1660s until 1702. To the left of this house, at the end of a row of buildings, is the Grade II listed Mansfield's Unitarian Church. Its lovely interior reflects the huge support that Nonconformist sects enjoyed throughout the country in the eighteenth and nineteenth centuries.

Erected in 1702, it is a direct result of 200 years of religious turmoil in Europe. This turmoil was itself a major cause of the English Civil War and the regicide of Charles I. The building is the oldest Nonconformist church in the county and one of the oldest in the country. It serves as an excellent illustration to the fascinating story of religious dissent in Britain around that time.

Two years after Cromwell died in 1658, King Charles II took the throne. Despite promising to be tolerant, Charles passed a series of Acts, including the 1662 Act of Uniformity, designed to punish Puritans. It was a decisive moment in the history of English Protestantism. Over 2,000 clergy lost their jobs because they refused to submit to the Act's terms. Charles piled the pressure onto the Nonconformists by making meetings of five or more people for worship unlawful, and by banning ejected ministers from a five-mile radius of their former living or incorporated town. This 'Five Mile Act' brought the Nonconformists to Mansfield because it had not been incorporated as a town by Act of Parliament. So, dispossessed ministers from Nottinghamshire, Lincolnshire and Derbyshire came to the town to minister their congregations in secret. (Robert Porter's Old Parsonage became one of the houses where the dissenters met.)

When Charles II died, James II attempted to reinstate Catholicism. He failed and had to flee the country in 1689. In that same year the new monarch, King William III, attempted a compromise by passing the Act of Toleration. This permitted the Nonconformists to worship freely in their own way in their own chapels and meeting houses. Increasingly over the next 150 years they did just that and, by so doing, changed the face of religion in the country. It has been estimated that between 1689 and 1710 nearly 1,000 meeting houses were erected. In Nottinghamshire, 51 places were licensed for dissenting worship within ten years of the Act, including two in Nottingham – since demolished. By 1851 a religious census revealed there were almost as many Nonconformists as Anglicans in England (whereas in 1689 the great majority of people were members of the established church).

This site opens up the stories of the Reformation, the Dissenting movement and the Puritans. From one Puritan congregation, founded at Scrooby (North Notts) in the early seventeenth century, several families emigrated to Holland to escape persecution. Some of these then joined the Pilgrim Fathers on the *Mayflower* in 1620 (see A.C. Wood, *A History of Nottinghamshire*, pages 163-64).

There is a coffee morning every Saturday 10 a.m.–12 a.m. where visitors can obtain information about Unitarianism or the site itself from friendly people who will just answer your questions.

Other titles published by The History Press

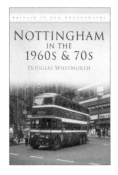

Nottingham in the 1960s and 70s.
DOUGLAS WHITWORTH

In the 1960s the citizens of Nottingham saw the greatest change in the city in the twentieth century. Many slum properties were demolished in the area around Walnut Tree Lane near the castle, but a number of historic buildings were also swept away in the construction of the new road – notably Collin's Almshouses and St Nicholas' Rectory. The construction of the Broad Marsh Shopping Centre was equally contentious. Featuring over 200 photographs from archives and local people's collections, this book is guaranteed to be of interest to anyone who has ever lived in or visited this great city.

978 0 7524 4887 9

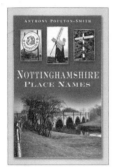

Nottinghamshire Place Names
ANTHONY POULTON-SMITH

This dictionary of Nottinghamshire place names examines their origins and meanings. It includes not only towns, villages and hamlets, but also rivers, streams, hills, fields and woods, as well as streets, buildings and public houses. A comprehensive description of the origin and evolution of each name is given, which brings to life the history of the place in a new and remarkably revealing way. Few are aware of the background of the names that are part of our everyday language, and Anthony Poulton-Smith brings this aspect of Nottinghamshire's rich history to life.

978 0 7524 4888 6

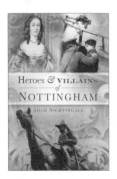

Heroes & Villains of Nottinghamshire
ADAM NIGHTINGALE

This fascinating collection of biographies chronicles the lives of some of Nottingham's most famous (and in some cases infamous) personalities. Inside these pages, you will find Civil War legends such as Colonel John Hutchinson, naval adventurer Edward Fenton and Victoria Cross winning air aces, as well as brave soldiers who fought against enemies as varied as the Zulus, the Spanish, the Confederates and the King. Illustrated with over eighty pictures this book is a must-read for all those interested in the history of Nottingham.

978 0 7524 4924 1

Haunted Nottingham
ANDREW JAMES WRIGHT

Andrew Wright – a local spectrologist – gives talks on the investigation of alleged paranormal activity and has thirty years of ghost research under his belt. His previous titles include *Haunted Leicester*. This collection of stories of apparitions, manifestations, strange sightings and happenings in Nottingham's streets, churches and buildings will delight anyone with an interest in the paranormal heritage of the city.

978 07524 4194 8

Visit our website and discover thousands of other History Press books.

www.thehistorypress.co.uk